D1178636

Do You See What I See?

How to Adjudicate Theatre Festivals

Annette G. Procunier

authorHOUSE®

AuthorHouse™
1663 Liberty Drive
Bloomington, IN 47403
www.authorhouse.com
Phone: 1-800-839-8640

First published by AuthorHouse 6/2/2010

ISBN: 978-1-4490-6701-4 (e)
ISBN: 978-1-4490-6700-7 (sc)

Printed in the United States of America
Bloomington, Indiana

This book is printed on acid-free paper.

With Thanks to Sherman and Ann Ward

Introduction

Adjudication has long been part of theatre festivals world wide and although there are many different ways to approach it there are some fundamental truths which make the process meaningful for the participants and the audience. This book is intended to outline for both those wishing to become Adjudicators and those who participate in festivals some of the elements that make for a good adjudication.

At its best adjudication can be a positive learning experience for both the participants and the Adjudicator. It has evolved from being a purely judgmental and critical evaluation to an opportunity for the exchange of ideas, knowledge and experience not only about a particular production but the theatre as a whole.

The aim of this book is to help anyone wanting to become an Adjudicator to understand what the basic skills are that need to be learned and mastered and to be a guide about how to know what to do in different festival situations.

For those who are already Adjudicators it is intended to help to refine your skills and to give a more in depth look at the theory as well as practice of adjudication at its best and to perhaps give you key points for improving your existing abilities.

If you are looking to organize a festival this book should help you to understand what an Adjudicator can and should do for your festival and how to choose one. It can also help you to understand how to use the Adjudicator to facilitate learning and create high standards at your festival.

For those who read it to learn more about festivals and what they are experiencing while listening to Adjudicators it is intended to give you a benchmark for what you should expect from the adjudication process.

In this book, besides giving the fundamentals of how to go about adjudicating theatrical productions there will be an in depth look at the components of theatre that should be addressed and why, along with some key elements of how to evaluate the success of a production versus reviewing or simply critiquing it.

Adjudication involves much more than expressing likes and dislikes as one would do when reviewing a production or providing critical analysis of the script and production in a non comparative way as can be done as part of theatrical criticism. Adjudication implies judgment and in the arts has come to be accepted as a comparative exercise with an element of competition among performers.

This exploration of adjudication is coupled here with a more academic look at what makes up a theatrical experience and how to separate the roles of the playwright and performers when evaluating the success of a production as well as how to judge the application of theatrics as seen on the stage.

The information complied here comes from years of adjudicating festivals in several countries, in situations both competitive and non competitive as well as from many teaching sessions for those wanting to become Adjudicators and for festival participants wondering why they should be adjudicated and what to expect from it. Although it focuses primarily on the process used for festivals by the American Association of Community Theatres it provides fundamentals which can be applied to any festival anywhere.

It is not intended to be a history of adjudication but rather a guide of how to adjudicate to improve the quality of theatre produced by the dedicated people who make Community and Educational Theatre a worldwide compelling artistic statement.

What Adjudicators Do

Adjudication can add a number of dimensions to a festival which will make it a more rewarding experience for all participants. Most importantly it can teach and encourage theatre artists to reach higher levels of excellence. Besides providing a context for the productions being seen which helps to establish their level of excellence Adjudicators can help the audience and participants to understand more about the types of theatre, playwrights and productions they are viewing.

The best Adjudicators possess a developed skill which emerges out of their love of Drama and Theatre coupled with a demonstrated aptitude for presentation and assessment and a desire to impart knowledge to others about this complex art form.

Often Adjudicators are chosen for their knowledge, their profile as artists and/ or their willingness to express their opinion. Although each of theses reasons has merit they will not of themselves be enough. Adjudicators must clearly understand the role they play in shaping the mood of the festival and an environment of non confrontational challenge and learning for the participants. Besides being a judge an Adjudicator must be a facilitator and teacher.

Several factors will help to enhance an Adjudicator's skill in imparting knowledge. Some of the most important are strong verbal communication, preparedness, objectivity, organization and credibility.

An Adjudicator must be focused on dealing with the important elements of the production to be evaluated. These include such things as integrity to the script, production values, interpretation, performance quality, degree of challenge and credibility.

It is incumbent upon the Adjudicator to use all these elements in forming an opinion and expounding upon it and in the case of a competitive festival judging the merits of one production versus another.

There are two methods which have been proven particularly effective in framing adjudication. One is the British Drama League System or as it is now called the All England Theatre Festival which assigns a measurable point value for acting, production, presentation and endeavor and is an excellent tool, particularly for novice Adjudicators in a competitive environment. Productions are rated using 40 points for acting, 35 for production, 15 for stage presentation and 10 for endeavor. [1] The system provides a built in organizational framework from which to work but may tend to make you too concerned about fitting your impression into a defined parameter rather than allowing for an evaluation of a work as a whole. Its strength is its structure and its weakness is its structure.

The second system, more widely used in the United States for Community Theatre Festivals is the American Association of Community Theatres Criteria for Consideration [2] which details 10 factors to be evaluated when adjudicating any production. Although there are no point values associated with the ten criteria they do provide an excellent guide for assessing the merits of any production and allow for comparison of work from different genres within a festival. Each of the criteria will be covered in detail later.

---

[1]   www.aetf.org/uk

[2]   AACTFest Handbook, festivals@aact.org

In keeping with the more contemporary approach to adjudication which focuses more on education rather than competition one may choose to be more eclectic in form with less emphasis on structure and a more interpretive response providing that all important production elements are covered.

As Adjudicators are often asked to compare productions of unrelated types of theatre such as musicals, drama and comedy it is critical not to lose sight of the value of the production as theatre and its total impact as opposed to judging the success of the separate elements used to create the whole. By doing this you will be able to measure the quality of productions of different genres using the same criteria of acting, directing and design for instance and assessing how they have affected the overall outcome. More about this later.

People want to be adjudicated for all kinds of reasons which often boil down to recognition and reinforcement. It is a truly professional Adjudicator who can achieve the delicate balance of reward with encouragement and meaningful critique.

Festivals are clearly meant as a venue of celebration of achievement and as an opportunity to explore new possibilities among people with a common understanding and objective. Theatre people are surprisingly similar worldwide and their reasons for producing plays are the same. It is a universal art form celebrating culture and the human condition and allows Amateurs and Professionals alike to express their joy in performing.

There is considerable debate everywhere about the role of competition in festivals. There are those who feel it stifles creativity in favor of winning and conversely those who feel it stimulates greater imagination among those striving for excellence. Some feel art should not be judged even though it is a common practice in all performing arts, even professionally. Regardless of the merits of competition most festivals have a competitive element to them and the Adjudicator must be able to balance the role of teacher and judge.

A good Adjudicator is as critical to the success of a festival as is the quality of the productions being presented and learning how to adjudicate well is a complex pursuit combining talent, knowledge, passion for theatre and strong communication skills into a professional approach.

Adjudication can be personally rewarding for the Adjudicator while giving participants the opportunity to learn, excel and commune with their fellow thespians. It is a role which must be taken seriously and requires training and practice to be effective.

To be an Adjudicator requires patience, keen observation, a practiced eye, fairness and a willingness to be exposed to new ideas. It will always be subjective in as much as there is room for interpretation but in the hands of a good Adjudicator adjudication can be a valuable tool for improving the quality of the theatre being produced and the understanding we have of it.

All of this being said we do it because people want feedback about their performance and with a good Adjudicator that feedback can stimulate people to achieve more and to gain confidence and grow in their work.

Drama, Dramaturgy and Theatrics

Everyone who watches a play has an opinion about the quality of the production. No matter how inexperienced we are about the theatre we all watch plays and pass judgment. Often that judgment is instinctive and based on whether we liked the play or not rather than on the production's quality. An Adjudicator is charged with a responsibility far greater than simply passing instinctive judgment. There is an expectation of expertise and understanding that will aid the audience to increase their comprehension of what they have seen and for the participants to help improve what they may do in the future. To do this the Adjudicator must evaluate the quality of the production elements rather than simply passing judgment on how good the play itself is.

In order to establish a strong foundation for any adjudication it is necessary to have an understanding of three separate components of the Theatre. They are Drama, Dramaturgy and Theatrics.

Drama is defined as "A term applicable to any situation in which there is conflict for theatrical purposes, resolution of that conflict with the assumption of character" [3] or "A poem or composition representing a picture of human life and accommodated to action"[4] Essentially Drama refers to the

---

[3]   The Oxford Companion to the Theatre Edited by Phyliis Hartnoll 1983

[4]   The New Webster Encyclopedic Dictionary of the English Language 1980

action or conflict and the text in which it has been placed. This could be a play, monologue, opera, musical, pantomime, collective, or improvisation to name a few.

It is not the role of the Adjudicator to place a value judgment on the quality of the script being presented. That is not to say that the script will not have a significant bearing upon the success of the theatrical experience but an Adjudicator must always consider level of attainment of the script's intention above anything else rather than judging the quality of the play. An Adjudicator must be able to distinguish between problems created by the text and the quality of the performance. It can be argued that a poor script makes for a poor production and while it is certainly true that it makes it more difficult to achieve a good production a poor script can be brilliantly executed while a wonderful script can fall short of the mark due to an inadequate production. That is what the Adjudicator has to evaluate. Are the strengths and weaknesses of the performance due to the inadequacies of the play or the production? In any event there is absolutely no room for subjective evaluation of the production due to personal likes or dislikes of scripts. Understanding the construction of Drama and how it influences the outcome of the play is essential but it must never be confused with assessment of the quality of the production itself.

To achieve an understanding of scripts (Drama) an Adjudicator must understand Dramaturgy defined as "The science which treats of the rules of composing dramas and representing them on the stage"[5]. To put it more simply Dramaturgy is the art of creating plays. Drama is the action being portrayed and the use of Dramaturgy is what creates it. It is the craft of playwriting. Without starting with the dramaturgical background of a play the Adjudicator could provide a critique which is focused on the wrong things.

---

[5]   The New Webster Encyclopedic Dictionary of the English Language 1980

Understanding Dramaturgy allows an Adjudicator to understand plays.

Among the things to look at are scene structure, dialogue, conflict, character development, narrative line, plausibility, use of language and dramatic resolution. These structural elements are necessary in the creation of a "good" play. An Adjudicator should use the knowledge of the play to create the basis for the evaluation of the production and by understanding what problems are inherently in it this will assist the adjudication process.

Besides understanding the literary structure of plays an Adjudicator must also look at the other components of Dramaturgy which involve exploring and understanding context. An example of using Dramaturgical knowledge to help position a play within the lexicon of theatre would be in relating the mid 20th century emergence of the Theatre of the Absurd and how it influenced writers in the 50's 60's and 70's. A R Gurney used some of the basic principles of the Absurd Theatre in his play "The Problem". Approaching that play from the Absurdist point of view helps to make it more accessible to the audience. While reading "The Problem" you can see how Gurney was trying to use the device of taking a normal situation and having people react to it in what appears to be an abnormal way due to their lack of communication. This is common in the Theatre of the Absurd. People say and do things that on the surface appear crazy but if allowed to unfold naturally will in fact make sense. The characters have difficulty communicating within the situation. Absurdist Theatre is based upon the assumption that human beings cannot communicate[6]. Knowing that Gurney wrote the play in the early 1960's when the influence of the Absurd Theatre was at its height puts its writing into context for the time and helps the producers of the play to see it differently from Gurney's later writings which while still often dealing with lack of communication are sometimes more literal in their conventions.

---

[6]   The Theatre of The Absurd, Martin Esslin 1961

When adjudicating a festival it is advisable for an Adjudicator to read all the scripts and do as much research as possible about the playwrights and works being presented. A thorough knowledge of the work is critical to making a credible judgment of the quality of the production. This is not to be confused with having an artistic opinion about the play but rather establishing a working knowledge of the script and the genre it represents.

This is more difficult than it sounds. Adjudicators all bring their own area of expertise to the works being evaluated whether they are directors, actors, designers or teachers. It is not the role of the Adjudicator to impose artistic interpretation on the production but rather to judge the merits of the choices made by the group and the degree of success they have achieved with those choices. Did the production work? It is essential to keep an open mind about a production regardless of how many times one may have seen the play.

An Adjudicator needs to be prepared to discuss the play within the context of the Author's other works, the genre it represents i.e. farce, melodrama, morality play etc., and its historical context i.e. Greek Drama, Restoration Comedy, or American Contemporary to name a few.

Adjudicators must be prepared to use some of the contextual information in the public adjudication as it will help to educate the audience about what they have seen and inform them about why certain judgments have been levied. It will also help to demonstrate the Adjudicator's perspective rather than having it appear to be merely opinion.

If a play has been edited it is critical for the Adjudicator to read the entire play. This is the beginning point of the production and if the script has been altered so has the overall impact. Knowing the entire play helps to establish the playwright's intention and will aid in evaluating the success of the production as it is presented. In edited versions it can be difficult for characters to make believable transitions because the dialogue removed often contributes to character development. Truncated versions of plays generally keep the narrative line but eliminate motivation and character detail which may alter the outcome of the production. This is done to ensure the audience understands what is happening but it becomes hard for them to understand why. If the Adjudicator is not familiar with the entire play unsuccessful elements of the production may in fact be attributed to the play itself rather than the version seen and a wrong assessment can be made. Blame for a problem may be put on the dramaturgical construct of the play rather than the performers' choices or the editing.

It is necessary to establish why a play was cut. The play is too long, censorship, unavailability of actors or to give each performer and equal number of lines have all been cited as reasons to me. Needless to say some reasons are more valid than others. The Adjudicator has the right to use the editing process as part of the evaluation and should be prepared to demonstrate why the choice may not have been successful and if possible provide alternate choices.

This is very different than commenting upon whether it is a good play or one the Adjudicator likes. The Adjudicator's personal preference in plays is of no consequence to the festival and should not be aired at any time during or after as it could lead to the assumption that it helped bias the evaluation made. You never want to hear the phrase "Well the adjudicator didn't like the play" uttered by the audience.

Evaluating the use of the script falls under the dramaturgical and a good Adjudicator needs to have a working knowledge of play structure, historical context, cultural influences and language.

Besides a clear understanding of Drama and Dramaturgy an Adjudicator must have extensive knowledge of Theatrics "the art of staging plays and other stage performances"[7].

---

[7]   Dictionary.com

This is the essence of what an Adjudicator is charged with evaluating. The other two elements will help to inform the proper approach to the production but it is really the application of Theatrics that is at the core of adjudication. Although it would be impossible to be an expert in all components of Theatrics the Adjudicator must demonstrate competence across all areas as they pertain to the production being evaluated. It is necessary to distinguish between the influence of the director and the work of the actor as well as determining whether the design has hindered or enhanced a production.

By the study of Dramaturgy an Adjudicator knows the playwrights intentions and by the study of Theatrics knows how the actors and production teams brought those intentions to the stage. Theatrics includes acting, direction, design, character development and overall effect to name the most important. Later we will examine, using the AACT 10 criteria one of the best methods for evaluating the use of Theatrics. Each element contributes to the production and the overall impact can be determined by assessing each part.

Adjudication must be perceived by participants as an impartial assessment of their work with award giving reflecting the quality of the adjudication. If the adjudications have been high quality the awards given should not be a surprise. It is unlikely an actor will win an award if his work has been criticized while others have been praised. Adjudicators must be careful when critiquing a production that they not live to regret their words. It is true however, that when awards are collaborative because there is more than one Adjudicator that an award can be given for a performance that not all the Adjudicators agree is of high quality. It is unusual to have an award given if the majority does not favor it.

Adjudication must ultimately be about evaluating the quality of the production and assisting the participants to see the points being made as a learning opportunity. The element of judgment exists but needs to be expressed as an assessment of the choices made and not a definitive statement of right and wrong. Rewards for excellence are part of competition and can heighten the power of adjudication if they encourage and stimulate rather than create an elite sense of superiority.

Not all festivals are competitive but this does not reduce the role of the Adjudicator in judging. Judgment is after all part of the definition of the word adjudication. [8]. Judgment may simply be the evaluation of the work in a freestanding way rather than as a comparison to the other works presented although traditionally competition has been involved. Which ever way the festival is designed Adjudicators are judging the quality of the work and making their assessments based on what they know about the components of Drama, Dramaturgy and Theatrics.

---

[8] The New Webster Encyclopedic Dictionary of the English Language 1980

The Qualities of a Good Adjudicator

In the last section we looked at the knowledge and understanding that an Adjudicator must possess to be able to provide credible feedback to the performing company and the audience. Regardless of how the knowledge has been acquired whether through long experience working in the theatre or from an academic background it is necessary to have that basis from which to work. It is not however, the only prerequisite for being a good Adjudicator.

To be successful, an Adjudicator must have the ability to organize material quickly into a coherent presentation and be able to succinctly make points before a group of people who by definition may be sensitive to what is being said and prone to take anything as criticism. There are three qualities you need to have in order to avoid being seen as critical rather than constructive.

First, you need to be able to concentrate completely on the production and your own presentation and to be able to hear every word you say as you are saying it and build on it during your adjudication. This establishes credibility and prevents rambling and repetition and avoids wasting time in a very time sensitive environment. It requires strong verbal skills, a good use of language and mental agility. It is the foundation of any successful extemporaneous speaker. It will make you compelling and interesting during your presentation and ensure that what you say is clear and concise. It can be learned by having your presentations critiqued and by practice but it takes time and effort to focus on your qualities as a speaker and not just what you are saying.

The second characteristic is an ability to read the response of the audience whether it is the performers or the play goers and interpret their attitude toward what is being said. This is particularly true when delivering a negative message. It does not matter what you are saying if the audience is not listening. Being glib, condescending, or egotistical will immediately alienate your listeners. You need to reach out to them and establish that you are there to help their understanding not to lecture or criticize. If you make them feel stupid they will not care what you have to say. You need to show a sense of humor without resorting to stand up comedy as well as humility in that you understand that you are not above what is happening and that being allowed to adjudicate a production is a privilege for you.

Thirdly an Adjudicator must be able to demonstrate a true understanding of what Community Theatre is and how much it means to the lives of the participants. If this respect for the performers and their productions is not evident nothing that is said will be taken seriously. Adjudicators must understand that this is done for love of the art, not monetary gain and that each person involved is giving freely of their time and talent and may be novice or nervous and only just learning to explore their gifts. Personal criticism can be devastating. The best way to prevent the adjudication from becoming a personal attack is for the Adjudicator always to keep one thing in mind. Criticize the performance not the performer.

Later in this book there will be tips on how to develop some skills in presentation to assist you in becoming a good presenter but the characteristics noted here are necessary prerequisites for honing those skills.

Preparation

When actually getting ready to adjudicate a festival there is a great deal of work to do and many questions that need to be answered for you. Doing as much as possible in advance makes the festival easier. Most information can be provided before the festival starts.

The following is a sample list of potential questions.

1. Is the festival competitive or a showcase?

2. How many Adjudicators will there be?

3. If there is more than one Adjudicator will it be individual or panel style?

4. Will there be public and or private adjudications?

5. What are the time allotments for each?

6. Are there guidelines for each type of session?

7. Is there set criteria for adjudication such as AACT guidelines?

8. How many plays are being presented and what is the schedule?

9. Are plays being performed in more than one language?

10. Are awards being given and what are they?

11. Who decides who wins the awards?

12. Is the Adjudicator to provide a written report on each play?

13. Is the Adjudicator expected to do a workshop?

14. Will the Adjudicator be asked to do press interviews?

15. Are there VIP functions that the Adjudicator must attend?

16. What is the Adjudicator's role in the Awards ceremony?

Besides these questions about the festival itself it is necessary to establish the details of remuneration, expenses, accommodations and timelines such as when to be there and when to leave. Contact information is critical. Find out how and when you will be paid. If you can claim travel expenses up front then do so. Find out if the festival pays mileage to and from your home to the airport and parking etc. Do not be afraid to ask questions around these issues as it is a professional relationship and should be entered into in that way.

An Adjudicator needs to be prepared to provide an up to date biography and photo for publicity and programs as well as receipts for travel costs. You also need to give the organizers any information about special needs such as allergies or diet. Adjudicators should also look professional and dress in a manner which reflects their own style but shows respect for their position and the festival. If there are dressy occasions such as awards ceremonies that you will be attending ensure you have brought appropriate clothes for the party.

Most festivals will send scripts in advance. All scripts should be returned at the end of the festival in the condition in which they were received. Some festivals will also send newsletters or brochures or provide a link to a website to help position the festival for the Adjudicator especially if it is your first time there. Take the time to read everything received. It will pay off as the festival progresses. Context is important in helping to keep comments positive and productive.

A new festival with inexperienced participants needs to be treated differently from one which has been running for years and has a very set method of operating. A new festival may benefit from guidance provided by the Adjudicator on how to make things easier. Do not provide any advice unless asked and then only after the festival is over. It is critical to remember that the Adjudicator is a guest of the festival and for all intents and purposes an employee and you need to respond in this way. Understanding the rules of the festival will help to avoid missteps, mistakes and hard feelings.

Know the festival timetable well. Make notes of how many plays are in each session and what they are. Know what other festival functions it is necessary to attend. Keeping a balance between free time and work is important as it is easy to become overtired when so much concentration and energy is expended in the adjudication process. Sleep is often at a premium especially if the Adjudicator is expected to attend social events.

Where ever possible Adjudicators should make their own travel arrangements. Sometimes festivals will want to do this for you for financial reasons but they are not always experts on airports and routes that work best for you. Transportation from airports should be established in advance with cell phone contacts in case of delays. Know the details of traveling especially if it is into a foreign country for you. For instance, if traveling into the United States by air it is necessary to have the exact address of the accommodation whether it is a hotel or private home and a valid passport.

Generally once the Adjudicator arrives there is a briefing session to cover rules, meet fellow Adjudicators and festival teams like timers and hosts etc. If it is a foreign language festival and the adjudication will be translated this is the time to determine what that process will be. Will each Adjudicator have a translator or will there be different translators who rotate? Does the adjudication time include translation or is that over and above the allotted time?

Annette G. Procunier

Establishing about award criteria should be done at this time as well with as much detail as possible about the intent behind each award and what your involvement will be in the awards ceremony.

You may be asked if it is permissible to record your comments either by audio tape or video. It is your privilege to say no however if there is not going to be a private or written adjudication you may be willing to permit it as in the "heat of the moment" immediately after the production some things may be lost to the participants.

A tour of the theatre is necessary. Find out what room has been set aside for Adjudicators and where the washrooms are. Ask for water to be provided that hopefully you can take into the theatre with you. Ask where the adjudication will take place, stage versus auditorium floor for instance and whether microphones will be used.

Choose your seat in the theatre. Choosing a seat well is an essential part of preparing for the adjudication. Ensure that there is at least one seat vacant beside you and that you feel you have plenty of room. You may want to have a vacant seat in front of you so you have no difficulty seeing and one behind you incase you encounter people who would rather talk than watch the production and thus distract you. You should also choose a seat that will allow you to exit the theatre easily after the show because you will need the time to gather your thoughts and climbing over a lot of people will be a struggle for you and them.

Most festivals will provide a clip board, pen, paper and a light. Some will provide a basic form for making notes often based on the British Drama League system which covers Acting, Production, Presentation and Endeavour or the AACT criteria. There may also be a place to note award eligible performances. Regardless, note taking needs to be simple and easy to interpret later.

For each session take the scripts to the theatre, have a program, a note pad and pens, and a light if taking notes. In order to not distract those around you use as small a one as possible. Be sure to have everything you need before the first production starts.

Under all circumstances be flexible and prepared. There are many pressures at any festival and the Adjudicators should not create problems for the organizers. Be on time, be ready to change if necessary, accept advice from the festival committee around things like using a microphone to be heard or going overtime etc and if you have grievances keep them to yourself until the end of the festival. Do not be afraid to ask questions if you are not sure about how something will be handled.

How to Watch a Play

Be seated in plenty of time to read and notate the program. Some festivals in the AACT environment may insist the Adjudicator watch the stage set up while others do not. There is no rule in AACT which dictates this. In other types of festivals set up may be done before the audience enters the house. Establish beforehand which way it will be. The setup should however, never influence any evaluation by the Adjudicator. It is the purview of the Festival Stage Manager to judge the set up and strike and often there will be an award for this given by the Festival Stage Manager. In many festivals the set up has taken on a performance life of its own which although good does not have any bearing on the outcome of the adjudication which centers on the performance of the play.

Be conscious of your initial impressions of the visual, audio and emotional while watching the production. It is necessary to evaluate the entire production and these elements are critical. Do not look for something to criticize. Watch the play as any audience member would.

It is crucial to find a reference point from which to work. This will be some component of the production that makes it work as an entire piece of theatre or conversely fail. It will be necessary to evaluate individual elements but the overall impact is the most important component of production. A production can be well crafted but still not have the required overall impact. An example of this happened in an International festival I adjudicated where a Russian production about the decent of Stalin into madness was presented. It was well acted and very clever in its production values with each element having been very thoughtfully executed. One of the points being made by the script was how cruel Stalin was and the director chose to use film clips from 1930's Russia to demonstrate this. Although it was effective in doing so the mechanics of raising and lowering the screen took the watcher out of the action of the play. Stalin's cruelty was ably demonstrated theatrically by his physical and emotional violence toward the other characters on stage and the use of the descending screen with clips removed us for the illusion of the crypt under the Kremlin where the play was set and sent us to the movie theatre newsreel. This disturbed the dramatic momentum and seriously detracted from the overall impact of the production.

By following one's instincts that something is not right rather than actively looking for production problems it is easier to keep the entire production in perspective. As you watch it will become clear what the problem is because the issue will be in evidence throughout the whole show. Look for what is very right and what is very wrong. Everything else on the stage will fall somewhere in between and you will have your reference point.

If it is necessary to take notes during a production it is counterproductive to take too many. Taking too detailed notes is simply repetitive and gets into minutia rather than allowing one to see the whole production. Note major concerns and examples of the concern but leave it at that. If, for instance, the blocking is poor note that and then forget about it. Belaboring a point causes imbalance in the overall assessment. Notes should be point form and represent highs and lows of the production. It is equally important to remind yourself of the high points as well as those things that are not working so well.

When taking notes it is easier to simply write one or two words that will jog the memory. For instance; polyester material is the note which means that the costumer is using the wrong fabric for the period. The note to the audience would be around attention to detail, poor design or research and the impact of anachronism on a broader level. The example would be polyester fabric for a suit on a character in a play in the 1930's.

Be sure to keep an open mind and not allow personal prejudices to color your overall impression of the piece. Certain playwright's works may not appeal to you but to allow that to cloud your judgment is wrong. You may not care for musicals for instance and would never willing go to one but that should not be apparent to the audience by anything you say on or off the stage.

Do not fall into the trap of seeing the play or role as you would have directed it or as you would have played the part. This blurs objectivity and results in a subjective assessment of the production. It is easy to watch a play and see it as a director or an actor and speculate on how you would do it or to compare it to other productions of the same play you have seen but comparison in this way is wrong. You are evaluating only what you see against the overall potential of the piece and not comparing it to other productions of the same work. These other experiences may give you a frame of reference for what is possible but they should not ever be mentioned otherwise the audience can conclude that your mind is made up about how it should be or that what they saw is inferior. Each production you watch must be viewed as if this is the first time you have ever seen the play.

Often plays are performed over a period of years at several festivals so it is common to see a play many times. You may even see the same play more than once in a festival. That cannot influence the assessment of the production being evaluated. Try not to anticipate the action or your response to the play because you are very familiar with it. It must be judged on its own merits with as fresh an eye as possible. You will be amazed how often you can be surprised by a play you have seen many times. Something will always be new.

Likewise if you have been adjudicating for some time you may see the same performers or companies on many occasions. Never assume that past success or failure will in any way be a reflection of what you are going to see. Letting the audience know that you are familiar with a company or their work will smack of favoritism. Personal references should be avoided.

Personal likes and dislikes around style should not enter into evaluation. The adjudication should be based on the application of theatrical elements and not personal taste on the part of the Adjudicator. Many people dislike Shakespeare being performed in modern dress but that opinion should not interfere with an objective analysis of how well for instance, the costumes were executed and how well they helped the audience to understand the play. Were they visually interesting? Did the period represented make sense in the context of the play? Was it represented accurately? These are the questions to be asked. Not did I like it.

Be aware of cultural differences and how they may affect an overall production. The Irish are noted for their beautiful use of the English language. They will usually bring this quality to any play regardless of its origin. Other countries like Japan have a strong visual tradition in the theatre and may be expected to bring that to their productions. This is not to say that concessions should be made for flaws or weaknesses because it is not part of their tradition but it is critical to keep in mind that there is more than one way to tell a story.

It is tiring to watch a number of productions in succession so keep your approach simple and allow the overall impression to be the most important component of your adjudication. It will be easier to keep everything straight. Above all else watch like a member of the audience and enjoy the show.

What to Watch For

This section looks at a basic structure which will capture the most vital elements of any production. They may be good captions to use when taking notes and will help you to organize your observations and thoughts. They can be the foundation for any adjudication.

Technical

Our first impression in the theatre is invariable visual. When evaluating the visual always consider the use of color, texture, workability of the set, costumes and lighting as well as the consistency and balance of the different elements. Beyond being visually interesting sets, lights, costumes and properties must also be functional. A set that does not allow the actors to move freely and create time and place no matter how beautiful is a detriment to the production. If you cannot see the actors due to low light levels no matter how emotionally evocative they may be it is not practical and costumes that are too clean to be real to the moment or too hard to move in will distract the audience and the actor.

It is necessary to determine if the design elements evoke the appropriate environment. It is not always possible in the Amateur Theatre to find just the right set or prop piece and if it is needed to indicate a certain historical period it can be even more difficult. Watch for anachronisms. Anything that does not conform to a design or time period will confuse the audience and detract from the play. The watcher spends time trying to figure out what is intended rather than being able to readily identify time or place by the objects chosen. It takes the audience out of the action and puts them back sitting in the theatre. A good example of this kind of lapse in detail is the frequency with which men wear modern rubber soled dress shoes in plays set prior to when these shoes came into fashion. Immediately the audience sees the actor and loses sight of the character. This may seem like a small thing but it is this attention to detail which helps to have the visual components enhance rather than detract from a production.

Design elements should always add to a production and not be simply an artistic statement of their own. Sometimes in the theatre we see exceptional designs which in a sense are over complicated for the play. They may be beautiful works of art and well executed but they do not fit. An example of that which springs to mind for me is a production of "Blood Relations" by Sharon Pollock which is the story of Lizzie Borden. Specifically in the script we hear that one of the factors that led to the murders may have been the cramped, hot, dark and depressing house where they lived. Lizzie felt trapped. The set for a production I saw was airy and large with a sweeping "Gone With the Wind" style staircase. It was beautiful but completely wrong for the play.

Set design needs to enhance the production by allowing the audience to understand where and when the action takes place. It needs to be visually interesting while remaining functional. Doors need to work properly; furniture needs to be placed so that actors can move naturally and effectively. Props need to work and be accurate to time and place. The set should provide multiple acting spaces and allow the director to create interesting stage pictures. It need not be any particular type of design. It just needs to provide a place for the action to effectively take place.

There are limitations to the complexity of lighting plots in competitive festivals because each production is being performed with the same basic light plot and a limited number of specials or effects which can be added. How these are used is a true comparator from one production to another.

Unlike sets, costumes or acting the basic components are the same. It is easy to see which company has been able to use the basic plot and specials to the best effect. In the same festival you can see a range from basic acting areas being in shadow to brilliantly executed plots that enhance the production visually and emotionally and even appear to lead the action.

When evaluating lighting plots look for how effectively the lights are used to illuminate the acting space. Are there shadows? Are faces properly lit? Is the overall light level high enough to see the action? Added to this you need to consider does the light help us to understand where we are. Is it indoors, summer or winter, day or night? Does the light change with time? Are the color choices evocative of mood? These are some of the considerations that should be reviewed when evaluating how effective the design is.

As well as evaluating the design it is necessary to judge how well executed the plot is. Do the cues work properly? Are there too many complicated cues which are poorly done? If we are aware of the lighting than it is intrusive rather than effective.

Sound plots are an easy way to create mood and environment and are sometimes not well used in productions. Often an Adjudicator is judging the absence of sound rather than the actual sound choices being made. Many productions use little sound and do not create a plot to accompany and punctuate the action. When judging the use of sound there is three aspects to consider.

The first is the functional sound plot, such as telephone rings and off stage noises that affect the action and are called for in the script or necessary to the activity. They must be authentic and recognizable to the audience. We should never be in a position to wonder what the noise is or what it means.

The second is the use of music and ambient sound to create mood and draw the audience more fully into the environment. This can consist of theme music used at the beginning and end of the play, music to cover scene changes, outdoor noises like birds, wind and water, or an underscore that is used in a cinematic way to highlight important points. This kind of plot should not overwhelm action or interfere with the play but should draw us in to the action and help to heighten our emotional response to what is happening.

The third component to be considered is how well the sound plot is executed. Are the sound levels appropriate and is the quality of the recording good? There is nothing worse than hearing the recording rather than the effect. Part of this consideration is certainly how well a company uses amplification for musicals whether it is in balancing the band or amplifying the singers. Can we hear the singers over the musicians and are wireless mikes crackly and cutting in and out? Are all parts of the music in balance with each other? Good quality execution of sound effects is critical and when it is poor can be almost more distracting than any other poorly wrought technical element.

All the technical elements need to be evaluated but due to the restrictive nature of festivals they are not as important a consideration as acting or directing. Besides the time, space and equipment limitations, and technicians may not be part of the original crew of the production due to in house restrictions or the rules of the festival. Additionally some festivals particularly in the International environment will provide basic furniture and set pieces for traveling companies. The Adjudicator needs to be aware of this prior to the festival in order to minimize criticism of things which are outside the control of the performing company.

Acting

In nonprofessional productions acting can be of a more inconsistent quality than on the professional stage. This is principally due to lack of training in actors and not lack of talent. The lack of training may manifest itself in poor concentration, loss of character, lack of focus, poor character development, naturalistic as opposed to realistic performances poor listening skills and lack of motivation or dramatic intent on the part of the actor. The result of this is that the audience sees the actor and not the character.

Many amateur actors are immensely talented but are not capable of repeated sustained performances because even for the most talented their ability to "hit the mark" is purely accidental and not the result of theatrical training that allows them to reproduce character and action as part of their performance.

In amateur productions there can be one or two outstanding performers who "steal the show" and seem to carry the production. It is a pitfall that directors may succumb to by allowing this imbalance thus being unable to develop a uniform ensemble. This lack of balance can seriously alter a production's intent and cause a breakdown in communication with the audience. It highlights one of the principal roles of the amateur theatre director which is to teach acting. To create the required balance a director has to even out the skills of the performers between the experienced and the novice and the talented and the willing.

In judging individual performances an Adjudicator must consider the degree of reality that the actor brings to the role. Often we see the actor coming through the role and lose sight of the character in the play. The truth of the performance needs to be assessed carefully. Is the intent of the playwright being served by the actor? Has the audience's disbelief been suspended? Does the actor manage to transcend imitation, trickery, mimicry and stage convention to provide a realistic character? Does the actor disappear and the character appear for the audience? The actor must walk, talk and be like the character and not be himself upon the stage. Realism is not to be confused with naturalism. As Lee Strasberg says

"You're being natural but that's not enough. Natural I can see on the street corner. What we ask is that you be real. Art is both more beautiful and more terrible than life."[9] Regardless of the Adjudicator's belief in "the Method" as a system of acting the concept of realism as opposed to naturalism is critical in evaluating the quality of acting.

It is the responsibility of the actor to provide a realistic foundation upon which the dramatic action of the play can proceed. In order to do this the audience must be convinced of the reality of the character and therefore the believability of the situation in which he finds himself. Even in the Absurd Theatre of Ionesco and Pirandello for example, there is reality and truth in the characters. There in lies the humor of the situation. The British perfected the role of comic reality in Farce where there are believable characters doing unbelievable things.

Besides the more esoteric elements of acting an actor must also possess control of the voice and projection, and have versatile use of the language of the play. The conversation in the play must be real. It is dependent upon rhythm, focus and balance both in the way the actor uses his body and in the vocal quality and use of language. The audience should be able to sense the quality of the language even in a play performed in a foreign tongue. Although it is said "love is the universal language" in the theatre speech must be the universal language.

Amateur actors sometimes lack the ability to use the body as part of their acting machine. They can convincingly say the lines but do not use posture, movement and demeanor to create character as well. These elements of acting must also be evaluated. Does the actor behave like the person they are portraying or simply say the words? Is the character old or is the actor playing old?

---

[9]   Strasberg's Method as Taught by Lorrie Hull, S. Loraine Hull 1985

The Amateur Theatre can also possess the problem of not being able to cast a person who is the right age for a part and that may also lead to unconvincing performances. All of this must be taken into consideration when evaluating the acting. One might say "well it is the Community Theatre so allowances have to be made for not having the right person to play that part." Rather than challenging the acting in this case the Adjudicator might want to challenge the choice of play. If you cannot cast it should you do it?

It is the actors' and director's responsibility to provide focus in a play. The audience should be watching the right things. This is achieved by a number of elements including body language, eye contact, active listening and the commitment of the actor to bringing life to the character. It is not enough to say the lines. The actor must bring the lines to life and make them the method for conveying the action of the play and creating the conflict to be resolved. We have to believe the character is the person he says he is. The director must challenge the actor to be real and use his craft to create a unique and interesting person within the play.

Each actor must contribute to the dramatic tension and energy that is already on the stage and help to create climaxes of action and reaction that are the play's natural momentum. The audience needs to care about the characters regardless of how unsympathetic they may be. Even the villain must be interesting and only the actor can create that interest for the audience. The audience must respond to the character the way the playwright intended. They do not need to like a character but they must care about him.

If the actors become the characters the director can then use them to focus on the play. It will give the play structure and purpose. The playwright will then be able to tell us what is on his mind.

Direction

Often in Amateur Theatre the director is the person who could be talked into the job, has performed in the most plays or read a play he would like to see on the stage. These are not necessarily the best qualifications for the job but in the absence of a qualified director, Community Theatres often must make do with what they have just as they must with actors or other production elements.

It is easy when adjudicating to attribute problems in a production to the actors or technicians when they really belong to the director. A poorly conceived production will be a failure regardless of the skills of the performers. The director must have a vision and it is that vision we must see not the visions of the individual actors. The best direction is undetectable to the observer but provides the framework in which the entire production can develop.

The most clearly identifiable directorial flaw is poor blocking. When adjudicating look for how the actors use the space. Is the play interesting to watch? Do the people move naturally around the set? Are they hampered by restrictions placed upon their movements by furniture or unnatural action? Is the "business" believable? Are there compelling stage pictures? If these basic physical components are there they should be unobtrusive. Their success is measured by their obvious absence. They are devices which allow the play to unfold before our eyes but are not things we should be conscious of when we watch a play. Adjudicators on the other hand need to evaluate the effectiveness of these parts of direction in order to determine how well the entire production is working and to understand if a production is failing where the weakness lies.

Besides the basic elements of movement the director must create mood, time and place. Is the appropriate style used for the production? If it is a period piece do the actors use the conventions of the period appropriately, for instance do women sit with their ankles crossed rather than their knees in plays of the 1940s and 50s. We see the world as the actors create it for us and become immersed in that world. Our disbelief has been suspended. If we cannot isolate where and when the action takes place by the actions of the characters and the different production elements we will become confused and miss the point while we struggle with the anachronisms.

Has the director created a production which conveys the intent of the playwright? Has the subtext been clearly explored, understood and presented to the audience? Has the play achieved a normal climax? Is the play balanced? Sometimes a director conceives of a play differently than the playwright intended and the experiment although interesting can be destructive to the playwright's intention. Experimentation is good and a valid exercise but if the audience cannot understand what the playwright meant for them to know the experiment becomes about the creativity of the director rather than about serving the needs of the play.

In a production I saw the director chose to present "The Elephant Man" in the style of Brecht. By giving the production this presentational unemotional kind of focus the play lost its impact upon the audience. It became an intellectual exercise but the audience no longer cared about the characters. When questioned about this decision during adjudication the director made it very clear that it had been his intention to remove the audience from any emotion in the play and turn it into an issue play where the audience would respond to the play only on an intellectual but not an emotional level. He had achieved this absolutely but the Adjudicator faulted him for not allowing the audience to see the play as the playwright intended.

It is equally problematic if there is no clear directorial intention in the production. The audience is then left to construe from it whatever they want. As the actors will each be conveying their own intentions there will be no clear statement of intent and an unsatisfying production regardless of how good the script is. Direction must always improve the audience's access to the play.

Choice of Script

Although everyone has certain playwrights whose work they prefer over others it is not the prerogative of an Adjudicator to judge a production based on personal preference. It is appropriate however, for the Adjudicator to evaluate the choice of the script as to achievability, appropriateness for the company, degree of risk and potential and to be prepared to point out the production difficulties that may have occurred because of problems inherent in the script.

A group may have chosen to perform a play which is far beyond their capability because they like it or they have seen it performed successfully before but it is outside their skill as actors or technicians. What can happen in that case is the group may alter the script to suit their capabilities or ignore the problem areas. Needless to say the production will fall far short of its potential.

Likewise a group may choose a play that represents no real challenge because it is easy to do and can be prepared quickly and without a lot of effort. What can happen in these productions is that they become one dimensional and skewed toward the talents of the individual performers who will push too hard to make it interesting or believable because they are under challenged.

Often in festivals due to time constraints plays are shortened. As long as the playwright has given permission for this it is acceptable but it will create unique challenges as cutting plays is not as simple as just eliminating lines. The intent of the play can be lost or altered in the cutting. This happens because the editor leaves in the plot elements of the play and removes character development or description that will help the audience understand the motivation of the individuals. The result can be a production which makes narrative sense but appears unmotivated. Why do the characters do what they do? Often the answer lies in what we did not see.

Sometimes plays are altered due to censorship. Companies fear reprisals from the audience if sexual or religious content is presented. Some festivals have strict rules forbidding censorship but it still happens. It can for instance, destroy the speech and rhythm of a play when the swearing, sexual innuendo or religious profanity is removed. It is hard to imagine a David Mamet play without the swearing and profanity. There would not be many words left. More importantly the core of the writing style and language would be gone as would the nature of the characters about whom he is writing.

Always an Adjudicator needs to be prepared to discuss the impact that cutting a play has had on its performance. It is necessary to distinguish between problems in acting and directing and problems presented by a changed script or a poorly written one. Sometimes the writing makes it impossible for the production to succeed as the basics of the play are just not there. This evaluation is different than judging the reason for the cutting. It is not appropriate for an Adjudicator to air an opinion on censorship or any other motivation for editing a play. All that is appropriate is commenting on the result to the overall production.

Community Theatre is a breeding ground for new plays and that is a wonderful role it plays in this day and age when Professional Theatres may feel unable to take a risk on a new show or do not have the money to have writer in residence programs which develop new plays for them. New plays have a place in festivals but if the play has caused the production to fail the company needs to evaluate whether it is appropriate to bring it to the festival in the first place. Organizations at times will sponsor new play festivals and then there is a great opportunity to discuss with playwrights and performers what works and does not work in the play.

Sometimes companies will choose to present a new play because it is the work of one of their members and they wish to support that endeavor. This is a good thing to do but the group needs to evaluate whether the script is of good quality or ready for production. This can be a sensitive area for Adjudicators because the writer can often be the director as well. In criticizing the production the Adjudicator will need to determine which part of the work is being evaluated, the directing or the writing. The production may not be successful because the play is underdeveloped or it may not be successful because the director is too close to the work and does not direct it well. It is hard to wear two hats and serve each part of the process well.

All these things are a completely different discussion from whether or not the Adjudicator likes the content of the play. Distinguishing the differences between a good play and a bad one and one that is in development is crucial for an Adjudicator. The Adjudicator needs to be prepared to address the elements of the play versus the production and how that affected the outcome of the piece. When discussing the problems the script may have presented the Adjudicator must be clear that although it may be a criticism of the play or its cutting it is not a reflection of personal bias but rather an explanation of why a production may not have succeeded.

Ultimately the choice of the play being produced and the reason for the choice are within the purview of the performing company and the Adjudicator is charged with evaluating how successfully they produced the play they chose. Knowing why a production is not successful is the role of the Adjudicator but knowing why they chose to do what they did will remain a mystery.

Overall Impact

Using the four criteria listed above an Adjudicator can evaluate the individual elements of the production and their affect on the overall performance. The elements individually will not determine how well achieved a production is but the accumulative effect of them will. At the end of the day overall impact will overrule a lot of individual concerns about the different production elements.

Adjudicators must first and foremost evaluate overall impact. It is unlikely you will ever see the perfect production and often ones that have serious flaws will still have a significant impact upon the audience because the basic elements are there. The power of the acting and the truthfulness of the interpretation will draw the audience into the play and have the desired effect on the audience. You can be left weeping at the plight of characters even though the set does not quite work or the costumes need to be changed.

The question can be asked if over all impact is the most important consideration why spend so much time on each separate area? Theatre is an accumulation of a number of different components which each contribute to the overall production and using the four criteria discussed above they will help to identify the good and bad elements of a production. This is vital for providing feedback to the audience and participants and helping them to understand the need for each part to support the whole.

The one over arching consideration when judging overall impact and the reason for the success of a production often comes down to attention to detail. If a performance shows the same even hand and quality in all areas of production it will rise to the top. It can be the smallest of things which separate a good production from a great one. The same quality and care have been given to all the choices in the production. This will create strong overall impact.

AACT Criteria for Consideration

Although there are many ways to evaluate productions and to organize comments for public, private or written adjudications the ten criteria established by the American Association of Community Theatres are among the best. They are a more in depth analysis of the four categories dealt with in the prior section and may help you to understand them even more. I want to cover the ten criteria completely here. They are comprehensive and allow for a close look at any production. Following them will provide for a fool proof process for adjudication. Keep in mind that these criteria apply to festivals of short plays performed in a bare stage to bare stage environment that of necessity does not allow for complex production elements such as elaborate sets and lighting therefore the focus is more on acting and directing. Nevertheless these criteria are valid for evaluating any production especially around the performance values.

The first criterion is, **"Is the acting believable and technically skillful with effective timing?"** This refers to the ability of the actor to suspend the audience's disbelief by creating character in a skilful rather than accidental way. The earlier reference to Strasbourg and naturalism versus realism applies here. Using this criterion one looks at the skill of the actor in using body, voice, and movement to create character and to command the stage and interact with the other actors. An Adjudicator would be looking for consistency in integration of talent and skill in the performer. Can we see the actor or just the character being portrayed? Are all components of acting used equally well? Often we can see actors who use voice and facial expression well but lack the ability to use the whole body to imbue character. A good example of this could be an actor portraying a much older character. The line delivery is convincing and the voice quality is good but the body movement betrays the age of the actor. He is not old but trying to play old.

This criterion does not cover how a character is interpreted and its validity in the production but rather speaks to the technical aspects of acting only. How good is the acting not how successful is the character interpretation?

"Are the characters well interpreted?" is the second criterion and an extension of the first one. Here the Adjudicator is looking for the combination of the actor and the director in creating characters that support the plot and playwright's intention. Have the right choices been made in creating the characters to support the play? Are the characters fully developed or only one dimensional? I once saw a production in which an actor gave his character exaggerated effeminate mannerisms which spoiled the resolution of the story about why an intended marriage would not go ahead. It did not come as a surprise to the audience when the engagement was broken off because the actor had given too many stereotypical clues early on as to the sexual orientation of the character. These clues were not in the writing of the play but rather in his interpretation. The result was to make the production unsuccessful because there was no suspense or conflict to be resolved. The end had been telegraphed from the beginning. The result of this kind of surface stereotypical interpretation was to cause the play to breakdown.

The acting can be technically skillful but the interpretation of the character sometimes doe not support the play properly as in the previous example. This may be the fault of either the director or the actor. Each person will see the character of a person in a play differently. Actors tend to work from a more narrow point of view because they are seeing what their character wants but not necessarily seeing what the playwright intended for the entire work. Focusing on only one point of view will cause even the most skillful acting to fail because the interpretation was wrong.

Criterion #3 is **"Does the company display ensemble work?"** This will show in how balanced the acting is among the performers. The old adage there are "no small parts" applies here. Each actor needs to bring equal skill and focus to his role or the production will become imbalanced with attention going potentially to the wrong character. Often people use the expression "He stole the show". This is a negative thing as it implies the actor was the centre of attention when he should not have been. A true ensemble piece will have a natural relationship among characters as a result of the seamless quality of the acting among all the performers. Each person is equally believable and in balance with the others and the play.

Are the actors listening to one another and responding as characters rather than simply reciting their lines with no reaction to the other characters? Listening drives character development through interaction and that is a major component of good ensemble playing. It also drives dramatic conflict in that characters are responding to what is being said and how it is being said. From listening comes character and believability. The audience will hear the words but if they do not see the appropriate response they will not believe what is happening or accept the characters. They will only see the actor. It is easy to spot an actor who is working in isolation and not really responding to the other actors. There will be a lack of spontaneity in the responses because the actor is simply waiting to say his line.

Other ways of evaluating the quality of the ensemble can be around how well the characters interact with one another. Are the relationships believable? Do the actors playing lovers respond appropriately to one another on all levels? I once adjudicated a comedy in which the characters were attempting to have an affair which got interrupted by all kinds of circumstances and never was consummated. The actor and actress involved were technically skillful, the comic timing was good and they had ably interpreted the essence of their characters however they appeared to not have any real physical attraction to one another. Turns out they were brother and sister in real life. No wonder they did not manage to convey the truth of their characters. They could not play successfully together on all levels.

"Is the material appropriate for the company?" which is Criterion #4 can represent one of the biggest challenges for companies. Plays are chosen for a variety of reasons.

Sometimes companies want to work on new plays which may not be fully realized and as a result create major production difficulties. This needs to be considered when judging the suitability of the piece for the company. If the play is underdeveloped the performers can still give first class performances but have an unsatisfying production. The performance is not the problem. When that happens Adjudicators must always remember they are evaluating the production not the play. It can be a tricky area of distinction. It is appropriate for an Adjudicator to point out how an underdeveloped script presents performance problems and by choosing to mount the play the company may have handicapped themselves from being competitive because they were not able to show their complete theatrical capabilities.

Companies will select plays they cannot cast due to a variety of reasons such as age limitations. They are more likely to be successful casting a play with younger actors playing older characters than the reverse however any significant age difference between the actor and the character will be problematic. Sometimes companies will change the sex of a character because they have more women then men in their troop. This may in fact skew the play badly as the nature of the interactions may change. Without permission of the playwright this is an unacceptable practice.

Theatre companies choose plays that require significant editing due to their own demands for censorship, time constraints or staging limitations. The result can be an unsatisfactory production. I once saw a production of a play that had been seriously altered to ensure that all three actresses had the same number of lines. This did not in any way serve the needs of the play but satisfied the requirements of the actresses to have everyone's part equal in size.

Companies may choose to do a musical because they are popular with the audience and sell lots of tickets but they do not have the voices or musicians to perform it. No matter how effective any other element of the production is a musical performed by people who cannot sing well is not going to be successful. Even one poor singer will adversely affect the ability of the company to have a high quality production.

Any of these issues along with a myriad of others will indicate that the material is not suitable to the company. It can be the biggest single problem a company faces and one of the easiest to overcome. Choose good plays that the director has a vision for and which can be cast without stretching the limits of credibility of the actors.

Sometimes Adjudicators are in a position to have to award best production to a skilled company doing a bad play. The challenge for the Adjudicator lies in determining where the problem lies whether it be the script or the performance. My advice to companies who are highly skilled and doing poor plays is always to choose a better play. If you are going to work that hard why not start with a good play

The fifth criterion is, **"Is the concept appropriate for the material and realized by the company?"** This can be a major stumbling block for theatres as festival productions are sometimes presented with a minimum of design elements or conversely a company may go all out in order to demonstrate how capable they are.

Companies may attempt to create something clever rather than appropriate to the action or playwright's intention in order to show their skill and they lose sight of the real reason for design which is to enhance the audience's understanding of the play.

Other times, at worst there is no concept at all but rather a mishmash of elements thrown together without coordination of the whole. Designers need to work together and there needs to be a coordinated effort. The Director needs to have a strong say in creating a concept for the whole production which balances the needs of the play with the creative talents of the designers.

On the other extreme the concept can be almost overwhelming in its design and detracts from the production. It becomes about showcasing the skill of the designers rather than enhancing the audience's understanding of the play. This kind of imbalance is as inappropriate as a lack of consistency in the acting. We are drawn to watch the wrong things.

Adjudicators, on a practical level need to evaluate the set design, lighting, sound, costumes, props, makeup and hair and how they work together. Attention to detail is a vital component for consideration in this category. Anachronism is also important for consideration. Do the pieces chosen represent what they are intended to be? Costumes which need to be period specific must be accurate and all the choices need to be consistent to the same period for instance.

Companies may choose to set plays in a different period or with cross gender casting or using mime and chorus or dance to comment on the action. None of these decisions is inherently wrong but if the concept does not suit the material and is poorly executed it must be dealt with in the adjudication.

If the design choices or lack of them do not allow the audience to better understand the production they have failed. No matter how well executed they are choices that confuse the audience or draw attention unduly to themselves will be a problem. The concept should enhance the play not detract from it or change the essence of what the playwright wants us to know.

"Has the structure of the production been controlled?" frequently presents the most difficulty for Adjudicators struggling to understand the criteria. It is criterion number six.

A play's structure involves the creation and resolution of conflict. This does not refer to fighting and anger but to dramatic conflict which is the purpose of the writing. Dramatic conflict is the actions and reactions of characters and how these actions affect others and the plot or intent of the play. It drives the action both in character and plot. The director and actors must recognize these moments and point the dialogue and action to support them. Not everything said or done in a play is of equal importance and the performers must guide the audience through the play. This is done by ensuring that each moment is allowed to exist of itself before moving on to the next. As a result of this, a production will be allowed to reach its climax and if the script is well constructed it should point to the playwright's intention.

The elements to be considered in evaluating structure are pacing, rhythm, narrative understanding, character development and overall believability of the situation and resolution. These are all discussed separately under acting and directing but the accumulative effect will be demonstrated here under structure. The evaluation of all of these components takes on a dramaturgical aspect under structure. By this I mean the theatrical elements of acting applied properly will help to inform our dramaturgical understanding of the play. The audience will see the conflict and the character rather than just the story being told. They will suspend their disbelief in favor of the author's world of the play and be absorbed in it. A successfully structured production will allow the play to disappear and the world of the characters to emerge.

In evaluating the acting and directing visually the point **"Are the movements and stage pictures effective?"** is the criterion. It is the 7th of the list. Besides creating character, pace, rhythm and structure a director needs to make the play visually interesting and effective for the audience. There needs to be a compelling visual world created by the actors not just the set and costumes.

Movement needs to be natural and uncluttered while being purposeful and interesting. It is a real skill to move actors effectively around the stage as if the space is home to them and at the same time keep the production from becoming static and boring. In real life people will sit for hours on a sofa and talk to one another but on the stage the audience needs some kind of movement which is in fact more than one might see in real life in order to maintain visual interest.

Besides creating believable movement it is necessary to create focus for the audience. We will watch what we want if the director does not point us to the most important action on the stage. We talk about actors upstaging one another. What that means is the focus has been taken away from the activity we should be watching either due to the antics of the actor or poor staging which has people in the wrong place or doing the wrong things. A common example of this may be action played behind the sofa which should be down centre for everyone to see. We see the sofa rather than the action. Another flaw we often see is furniture that obstructs the entrance to the stage and the audience cannot fully appreciate the entrance or exit of a character because they simply cannot see it without looking around or through something. Furniture placed in such a way that actors have to move unnaturally around it can be a problem as well. A coffee table that is too close to the sofa causes actors to shuffle in to sit down. The audience sees the actor and not the character when this happens.

Actors who move without motivation are another distraction as are actors who tend to shuffle or fidget when talking or listening. We see the actor and his mannerisms rather than seeing the character. Inexperienced actors will sometimes fidget and not even be aware it is happening. This nervousness may detract from the character and the audience will find their eyes moving to this superfluous action.

Stage pictures are very important to leave us images that impress points upon us. In musical theatre the very best productions have each musical moment punctuated by a completed picture at the end of the musical number rather than the song simply stopping. Lighting, movement and posing can create these images which help the audience to remember and focus on the moment.

In comedy it is often the physical actions which will heighten an already humorous moment. This is especially true of slapstick and farce. Timing is critical to make these moments work. It must appear spontaneous and natural and yet take the audience by surprise.

All of these elements are to be evaluated in "Are the movements and stage pictures effective?" A true test of the criterion would be can you take snapshots of the action and from them see if you can understand what is happening to the characters. When watching theatre in other languages this criterion is very important. Although we take language for granted it is a good test of successful theatre to try to watch the play as if you do not understand the language and see if it is still interesting and understandable.

The eighth criterion is **"Is the production well paced?"** A poorly paced play is generally the fault of the director. Maintaining pace and rhythm requires listening on the part of the actor and the director. Sometimes directors allow the mistake of seeing pauses as emotion or reaction and permit the actors to wallow in the action either milking for laughs in comedy or attempting to create great emotion in a serious play. It can be the result of inexperienced actors thinking "the pause" is an effective emotional response. Pausing for affect, as it is sometimes referred to is an unnatural stalling of the action. Any pause an actor takes need to be driven by the action and reaction and come naturally as a response to the situation not as something layered onto the scene.

In comedy it is necessary at times to "wait for the laughs" and this is a real skill in that the actor has to judge the time it takes for the audience to react to the action but not wait so long that the action stops and the actor loses focus and momentum. Likewise the actor cannot simply keep going over the laughter which neither allows the audience to react appropriately or to hear the next lines.

Sometimes pacing is confused with speed. In this case the actors simply race to the end and do not take the time to allow each moment to be resolved. This can happen in productions with time constraints which are cut too close to the running time. There is no time for audience reaction or character reaction so the actors keep going no matter what. The performers miss the "beats". In this case the production no matter how well acted will seem rushed.

Problems with rhythm are a result of poor listening. An actor is waiting to say his line and not responding to what has been said to him. He can pick up the cues properly but not infuse the lines with life. Each line is said as if it was memorized and not as if it is being said for the first time. The actor races to the end of the line and then waits for the next line. No matter what is said or how it is said the actor says the next line without any meaning. In this case the pace is fine but the rhythm is not and the result is lack of understanding of what is being said and a proper response to the moment. The expression "the actor is not in the moment" applies here.

Pacing and rhythm problems will destroy even the best conceived and staged productions no matter what the quality of characterization.

"Do the technical elements support the overall production"? This is criterion nine. As mentioned earlier in AACT short festivals the bare stage to bare stage concept is used so technical elements can be challenging or limited. Everyone is working within the same constraint but the Adjudicator does not know what the performers have to work with in their own theatre so it is important to judge only what is presented and how effective it is in enhancing the understanding of the play.

Choosing the right play can be crucial to the success of the festival entry especially in this category. Sometimes plays are presented which were not specifically chosen for festival competition but rather as a version of something already being performed in the festival participants' season. The two ideas do not always mesh. A play with an elaborate set or multiple scenes may be too complicated to bring successfully to a time limited festival. Lighting plots requiring a lot of specials and multiple cues may not work in a restricted environment.

Traveling with a huge show may also not be practical. Thought needs to be given to all these different requirements of the production.

Companies may have to present a version of a production that was staged in a different style such as thrust versus proscenium and they will need to alter the production enough to suit the new environment. The initial festival may have been held in a small venue and the play might after several levels of competition be performed in a very large house where the dynamics will be changed. The company must be prepared to adjust to these differences and make the production seem fresh.

Lighting capabilities may vary by house and with limited rehearsal time in the festival venue cues and levels may not be adjusted properly. A complicated plot could exist but it may not be possible to execute it effectively given the time if the operators are not skilled enough or given enough rehearsal time.

Sound plots can be very effective in enhancing productions and in my experience are sometimes used in too limited a way. Besides creating mood with theme music and underscoring sound can help to establish time and place such as the use of outdoor noises specific to times of the day or season which immediately tell an audience where they are even more effectively than visual clues. Another aspect of sound which requires consideration is how effectively amplification is used in musicals. Balance between the band and the singer is evaluated under this category as is the seamlessness of the use of microphones for the singers. Effective singing can be undermined by sound systems that are not working properly or body packs that are not adjusted well for volume.

This category, like lighting must be evaluated both for design and execution. How well does the design work and how well is it performed. Just like acting it can be ineffective if not properly performed no matter how well conceived.

Set designs need to be effective and not overwhelming. They need to be easy to change between scenes if required and allow the actors full range of movement while creating a defined acting space. The audience needs to accept that the scene has been properly set to allow understanding of what is happening. In festivals with time restrictions and space limitations the choices made can be critical to the success of the production. Often the audience is asked to accept a simple chair and table as representing the "room" where the action takes place and this is suitable as long as the pieces chosen in fact indicate clearly what we are to think. The acting space or "the room" may be defined by lighting or blocking which allows us to see a much smaller space inside a very large stage.

Two components of the technical which will not be affected by moving the show from one place to another are costumes and makeup/hair. These elements are transportable and should not be judged in any limited way. They can be the most fully realized technical aspects of a production in competition. Regardless of how simple the other components of the technical may be these can be used to bring the audience even more deeply into time and place by the authentic way in which they are used. I once saw a production of "Steel Magnolias" which is set in the beauty parlor where the creation of "Big Hair" is the specialty. None of the actresses had big hair and when I asked why not the director said they had chosen not to bring the wigs on the road with them. That was a poor decision.

The last criterion for consideration is **"What was the total impact?"** This is the most important thing to determine. No matter what details may be lacking or problems the production may have had it can still be effective in illuminating the playwright's intention and in moving the audience. The small details should not get in the way of the Adjudicator's ability to evaluate the overall impact.

When judging an overall production this is the deciding factor. How well was the play realized? Was it as effective as it could have been? Overall did the audience see the situation, the characters and the life of the play or did the lack of detail make them realize they were in the theatre and not in the moment? Did the overall impact of the production allow the audience to suspend its disbelief? That is the measure of total impact.

These criteria are comprehensive and simple to organize when watching productions and can be used in any festival environment. They do not have a point value system attached to them but can still provide a good framework for watching a play even if there is a requirement to assign marks to acting, directing etc. Once Adjudicators have a firm grasp on these 10 criteria they can adjudicate any kind of festival anywhere.

How to Present the Adjudication

Festivals provide for adjudication in a number of different ways. Typically there is a public adjudication held immediately after the performance of the play. The Adjudicator may be allowed 5 to 30 minutes to present their critique to the performers and audience both. Some festivals also allow for private adjudications which take place at another time and last anywhere from half an hour to 2 hours while other festivals will have an open forum the following day where all festival participants may attend and participate in the discussion. Some festivals also employ a feedback session after the award decisions have been made where participants can ask questions for clarification or follow up to something said at the public adjudication. There is no right or wrong way to provide adjudication feedback. The festival committee will determine what the method will be and the Adjudicator should be aware in advance of what format will be followed.

Adjudicators must be knowledgeable about Dramaturgy and Theatrics. They must be able to watch a production and discern which are the key elements causing its success or failure and be able to bring a dispassionate view to their judgment. They must be able to evaluate productions for their merits rather than simply the merits of the play and be able to compare the quality of different genres and theatre types when deciding best of, in any category of award. Most importantly Adjudicators need to be able to present their views to the participants and audience in a positive, organized and constructive way. In order to do this they must possess a number of positive qualities and be able to learn and hone the skill of presenting extemporaneously to a group after only a few minutes of deliberation.

Public Adjudications

Although Adjudicators are a key component of any festival they are not the "Stars" of the show. They are facilitators charged with making judgments on the relative merits of the productions. It is easy to fall into the role of entertainer rather than facilitator and that can be dangerous. It is necessary however, to develop a rapport with the audience in order to have people hear what is being said. If one is incoherent, repetitive or too aggressive the audience will not be receptive to what is being said. By definition the participants are expecting criticism of their work and it is a labor of love over which they have spent many hours and regardless of how it is viewed by the audience they believe it to be good and certainly the best they can do. To put it before an Adjudicator to be critiqued requires courage and more than simply the desire to win an award. They must be willing to listen and learn. The Adjudicator is responsible for the tone of the adjudication and for ensuring an environment of learning.

There are a number of keys to establishing rapport with the audience and ensuring an effective use of the time available. In AACT festivals adjudication is done on a bare stage after the production has been struck. The houselights are usually up and the cast and crew are seated near the front of the audience. The timer will be visible as well and timing signals should have been agreed upon before the adjudication starts. In other kinds of festivals the adjudication can be given on the stage with the set still in place or sometimes from in front of the stage. Sometimes the cast and crew are backstage and not visible to the audience or Adjudicator.

Regardless of how the stage is set it now belongs to the Adjudicator. Rather than simply standing still if not constrained by a microphone on a stand or a podium it is possible to move about the stage to demonstrate use of space, vocal problems or blocking choices. The audience is able to visualize the point being made if the Adjudicator moves into the space being discussed and describes the situation. Adjudicators should follow the same principles as actors. Don't shuffle or wander. Be careful of distracting personal mannerisms. Speak clearly and slowly. Stay in the light.

An Adjudicator should always speak directly to the audience as if speaking to one person. It is appropriate to elicit audience response by asking such questions as "Am I making myself clear? Or do you understand?" The intention is not to get into a dialogue with the audience but rather to establish an intimacy.

It is important to acknowledge the performers even if they are as noted earlier back stage. If the performers are seated in the audience then when speaking about a particular character the comments should be directed on a personal level to the actor. The audience will listen in on these exchanges. This is especially true when giving a compliment. If they are not in the audience make it clear which actor is being acknowledged.

It is easier to refer to a performer by the character's name rather than to attempt to use an actor's real name. This prevents confusion for the audience and the Adjudicator and saves time. It prevents people from fumbling in their programs to see who is being talked about. Where possible an Adjudicator should clarify visually who is who when greeting the performers at the start of the adjudication. People look different when out of character and it is important as well to know who the key production people are like the director and designers.

In a five to ten minute adjudication try to cover three to five main points both good and bad and be prepared to make specific reference to the show. For instance if the blocking needs work use an example from the show of how the blocking did not work. Once the point is made move on as time is limited and there is always lots to talk about. Likewise ensure that different elements are praised and why, again using examples from the production. It is not enough to say something was good or bad the participants need to know why otherwise it can be perceived as simply a matter of opinion and therefore subjective. It is also necessary to remember that the theatre is about choices so it is easier to discuss the choice made and why it did or did not work rather than saying something is good or bad or right or wrong. Although giving alternative choices to solve the problem is good it is not necessary as it is not the Adjudicator's job to redirect the show.

An Adjudicator should not make reference to another show in the festival unless it is to reemphasis some point being made on a theoretical level. For instance you might say "as I said yesterday consistent use of accents is necessary in any production". It should never be in comparison such as saying that the previous production did something well that this company did not. Never say anything about a prior production that has not already been said during its adjudication.

As a general rule it is important to balance the negative with the positive. Regardless of the quality of the production there will be both good and bad points. If the production is poor quality it may only be a moment that worked well or an effect that was successful but it will show respect for the work and the performers. It is easy when a production is not good to get mired down in the endless list of problems. Remember to speak about the production at the level where you find it. If fundamentals are not there like blocking and the actors cannot remember their lines it is useless to talk about subtle components of inner character motivation. It will be lost on them and not help them to improve from where they are.

An Adjudicator should refrain from telling a group they are wrong. Rather, it is possible to say a certain aspect of the production did not work for you. By doing this it is possible to suggest other choices that might achieve what the director was aiming for. Remember the very thing being discussed may have worked for others in the audience so the Adjudicator needs to be clear that it is an opinion but also one with reasons articulated around it.

Adjudicators should not dwell on any one area of production more than others especially if it is their area of expertise. This is very important particularly if what is being talked about is critical. Balance is necessary. The audience will have read the biography in the program and know what the background of the Adjudicator is but if that becomes the only area of focus credibility is lost and it appears that the Adjudicator does not really know anything expect their own area of expertise.

It is alright for an Adjudicator to say they enjoyed a play. Often Adjudicators in a competitive festival worry about tipping their hands and giving away who will receive an award. When this happens remarks may become critical, overly vague or noncommittal. The audience has their own opinion. They like to compare their perceptions with the experts. Sometimes in a festival there will be one or two stand out productions. Everyone knows it. It is acceptable to say that a production was outstanding provided it fits in the context of the critique being given. It is also acceptable so say that critical points being made about a good production are small because the production is high quality and there are not a lot of large issues to be discussed. Explaining why something is good helps the audience and other participants to learn about the theatre as well. Likewise a production may be very popular but not necessarily of the highest quality. When that happens it is also alright to be critical of that production and not shy away just because people liked it. Balance and fairness are what is important.

Adjudicators should not talk about themselves. It is inappropriate to reminisce about theatrical experiences unless they have something to do with the production. Refrain from saying "When I did this play or when I saw it last time" These kinds of remarks produce the automatic assumption that this production is wrong or inferior.

If it is necessary to use notes during the public adjudication do not be a slave to them. There is nothing more irritating than watching someone leaf through a lot of pages trying to find a specific note. If it cannot be remembered it is probably not that important. The notes should have been organized into a cheat sheet of a few points to be made rather than using the notes taken while watching the show. Stick to the larger issues and use the small points as illustration.

When the timer indicates a one or two minute warning it is critical to wrap up instead of trying to ram in a lot more information. The wrap up should touch on what was said and be sure to end on a positive note. If everything has not been covered so be it but do not rattle on and get disjointed or try too quickly to cover something. It is possible to make a mistake and say something you do not really mean.

If there will be a private adjudication at another time it is acceptable to hint at issues that will be discussed there. It lets everyone know that you are aware of what happened but that time may not allow for a full exploration of the point. It is then crucial to ensure that the subject is covered in depth in the private adjudication. Likewise you cannot mention every performer if you have a large cast play but you do have time to do so in the longer more detailed session. With the combination of public and private adjudications hit the high points of what you want to discuss in the public format and elaborate upon them in private as well as talking about other topics of lesser importance or which require more detailed exploration.

The key components of any good adjudication are being positive, constructive, helpful, respectful, concise and knowledgeable and remember to criticize the performance not the performer. Say what it is important to say and get off the stage. The Adjudicator is not the main act.

Forums and Private Adjudications

The private session is an excellent opportunity for the Adjudicator to elaborate on the remarks made in public and to properly explain what can have easily been misconstrued when emotions were running high after the production. These sessions are not generally as structured by the Adjudicator as public adjudications and can allow for dialogue and a more thorough examination of the production and the process.

It is a good opportunity for the Adjudicator to learn what drove the choices that were made and it should always be a dialogue and not simply an elongated lecture about what has already been said. Many topics that were not covered in the public remarks can be pursued in the private format. It is an opportunity to single out every performer which is important for their self esteem and gives balance to the comments. Remember the purpose is to critique but also to teach and encourage.

Initially allow the group to explain a little about their background and experience. Two key questions will open the dialogue. Why did you chose this play and tell me about your theatre at home. This allows the participants to talk first and establishes the rapport for dialogue. This also often helps to explain why certain things are the way they are. A company may be performing at the festival for the first time in a real theatre as opposed to the high school auditorium they normally work in. They may have chosen a certain play because they had the right actors for it or conversely because they really wanted to do it and stretched its credibility because they did not have the right actors. A director may turn out to be directing for the first time which could explain many shortcomings due to lack of experience. Establishing who is doing what for the first time is also important in order to know what to talk about and how.

If a production is seriously flawed due to lack of experience it will be necessary to assume a telling style of communication. The participants will be less able to provide suitable feedback because they just don't know or had never thought of things the way the Adjudicator is describing them. Always attempt to approach the company at the level they are rather than where the production should be. They may not be able to get where they should be due to lack of experience or resources.

In this situation discuss major problems with the production and do not be concerned about small things. If there is too much detailed criticism the cast and crew will become weighed down with it and feel that the problem is insurmountable. Where ever possible provide solutions or alternate choices. For instance if the set is small and cluttered with furniture thus restricting movement suggest rearranging or removing furniture. Often people feel they need all that furniture on the stage because that is what you would have in a real home. Coffee tables that separate actors from the audience and restrict movement are among the most common mistakes and the most easily fixed. Having furniture on the stage which is never used is another common problem.

It is possible to teach about basic stage craft in this environment like describing weak and strong spots on the stage. It will help to improve future productions and looks like help rather than criticism. It becomes an alternative way for the company to look at things rather than criticism from which they feel they must defend themselves.

When talking to actors ensure that the comments are not construed as a personal attack. Criticize the performance not the performer. Always temper the negative with something positive even if it was only a moment or one line that was well said. Leave the actor wanting to return to the stage.

While making technical suggestions remember the limitations of their normal working environment. It is counter productive to suggest cross fades to a lighting tech who does not have two dimmers.

Regardless of the resources of the group or lack of experience stress the need for detail. Often small things become irritating to the audience because no one bothered to care about them enough to make them right. No detail is too small and should not be overlooked. Often detail is what separates a good production from a great one. Stressing detail in the public adjudication will set the tone for the more intense discussion in the private format and certainly lets everyone know the Adjudicator has been paying attention.

Leave lots of time for questions. If the mood has been properly set to avoid criticism and foster learning there should be lots of questions. Asking if they understand what is being said also helps to determine the success of the session. It is critical to ask the group if there is anything that has not been discussed that they would like to know about. It is easy to miss someone or something and hurt someone's feelings inadvertently. Be prepared to respond to each question with detail and thoughtfulness. It takes courage to ask. If in fact people are having difficulty asking questions the Adjudicator can pose questions to them. For example, "Tell me more about ...." Will lead to the participants opening up and out of that can come their own questions. Give them time to formulate the questions as they are thinking about what has been said and may not feel sure just how to pose the question or express the idea they have in mind.

Good performances will often adjudicate themselves. Companies that are producing work at a high level have given considerable thought to the choices made and can reveal a lot about the process in a comfortable dialogue environment. Often the discussion about how the company got where they did is as interesting as what they did.

When an Adjudicator is fortunate enough to see such a production it is possible to take on the role of discussion moderator rather than lecturer. Encouraging the performers to elaborate on how they did what they did will allow them to do the teaching rather than the Adjudicator needing to do it.

Often they will reveal even more than was apparent in the production and that can be very interesting and enlightening to everyone.

When there are people other than the producing group at the discussion session they too can learn from the dialogue. The questions of the audience can help to add more complexity to the discussion. Often the questioner has an idea about something that they wish to share. It may be a different opinion than expressed by the Adjudicator and could be interesting to explore. It is up to the Adjudicator to control these questions and comments and not allow them to become a separate adjudication by someone from the audience. If they become adversarial or negative it is up to the Adjudicator to reestablish control of the conversation and direct the comments to another area of discussion.

Likewise a performer or director can become defensive about the choice they made and want to argue its merits with the Adjudicator. Although you want each person to be able to participate in the discussion it should not become an argument or an attempt by anyone to prove what they did was right. When it happens an Adjudicator can simply say "I understand what you were trying to do but that is not what I saw and that is what I am charged with evaluating". No matter what happens do not lose control of the situation. Do not belabor your point to prove you are right. You will never convince the person arguing of your correctness and will it will create greater tension and hard feeling.

When adjudicating over several days in an open forum where all participants may attend the sessions the Adjudicator may take the opportunity to vary the style of approach. Sometimes as suggested earlier it may be necessary to tell. Other times asking questions may allow dialogue to flow which the Adjudicator simply moderates and on other occasions the Adjudicator may in fact demonstrate what the point is by working with a few of the actors on a part of the play. As long as the director and actors are willing this can be a valuable way of showing rather than simply stating how different choices could change the outcome of the production.

Regardless of the style of presentation, it is incumbent upon the Adjudicator to retain control of the session. Sometimes companies will shut down or become argumentative. If this happens, move on to something else. It will not benefit anyone to get into an argument and it is not necessary for the Adjudicator to defend their position. It is after all a matter of opinion not fact. The adjudication is not the place to try to score points or establish who is right or wrong. It should be a place to learn.

The longer private or forum sessions are a good opportunity to teach about general principles of the theatre and not just to address specific concerns of the productions. Repeating themes throughout the festival and connecting them during the adjudications will reinforce the importance of what is being said.

Written Adjudications

Some festivals will ask for a written evaluation of each production to be provided to the company at the end of the festival or within a set time frame after it. This is sometimes done in lieu of a private adjudication. Establish beforehand if this will be required as it is considerably more work for the Adjudicator to do it. It is appropriate to request a higher fee for providing this material. It is common for the festival committee to provide a form for the Adjudicator to fill in which covers all the basic points of production. If there is no format provided it is more difficult to give a succinct evaluation of each production ensuring that all elements are covered equally. Where possible insist that a format be provided.

Do not attempt to fill them out during the festival. It is tiring and time consuming and will lead to an incomplete assessment. Make some notes to work from later and where ever possible elaborate on the themes covered in the public adjudication. It is possible to give lots of detail and to cover all the performers in this way when there may not have been time to do so publicly.

The danger in written comments is that the face value of what is written can be taken differently than it was intended and the tendency will be for the negative view to be taken. It is very important to be sure that the comments are a true reflection of what you mean and are as unambiguous as possible. They should always elaborate on things spoken about in the public or private adjudication and be as specific as possible. Unlike verbal comments in a private adjudication there is no opportunity for discussion or clarification and therefore there is more room for misinterpretation.

Be sure you know to whom the comments go. Often they are given to the director to share as he or she sees fit with the company. Sometimes they go to the festival committee who uses them to defend any disputes that arise after the festival. Either way it is important to know who the audience is for the material.

All the same rules around style apply to the written critiques. Keep them positive, succinct and well rounded.

Working with other Adjudicators

Although in some ways it is simpler to work alone one Adjudicator comes under intense scrutiny and the process of award giving can be perceived as very subjective. An Adjudicator does so much to set the festival tone that it is easy to misstep and have a festival fail. A weak Adjudicator will make for a weak festival. To avoid this many festivals will have multiple Adjudicators. These festivals do not generally have private adjudications although they may have a feedback session.

In American and International festivals it is common to work with one or two other Adjudicators. Hopefully they have been chosen carefully and will be compatible in style, personality and skill. This is not always the case and the audience may draw comparisons and choose favorites. It is a mistake to think that the only judging done at a festival is about the productions.

Commonly at AACT festivals Adjudicators are not permitted to discuss productions prior to voting on the awards. They are not allowed to listen to a fellow Adjudicator speak about the production before having made their own remarks. As a general rule not hearing another Adjudicator can be good as it does not prejudice your remarks. It does however sometimes result in considerable repetition for the audience. The positive side of this is that it is difficult to ignore an observation made by two or more people about the same thing. It can hardly be construed as only personal opinion if everyone says the same thing.

The downside for Adjudicators in this approach is that they cannot learn from one another either on presentation style or knowledge brought by their different backgrounds. A novice Adjudicator cannot benefit from being mentored by an experienced one. Adjudicators have no other peers at the festival except each other and it can be isolating without the benefit of discussion. For the participants it can also result in valuable feedback being dismissed because of a contradiction of something said by another Adjudicator. We all have a tendency to listen to the positive and dismiss the negative as wrong and contradictory adjudication can lead to that.

In non AACT festivals the rules about conversing with one another do not apply. Adjudicators often will discuss productions during the festival in order to get a better feel for what they each bring to the adjudication and to learn from each other. At International festivals Adjudicators typically come from different countries and have diverse cultural and theatrical backgrounds. It can be fascinating to listen and learn how each person approaches the work. As language is not the common thread in International festivals in can be enlightening to have another Adjudicator interpret the work in their way and to understand how their background influences what they see. It can be more revealing than the productions themselves in terms of learning about the theatrical traditions of a country.

When it comes to award giving in International festivals there is less structure to the selection process than is typical of an American festival and yet it has been my experience that each Adjudicator still has their own opinion and in the end there is still a degree of compromise as no two people ever see things the same way.

Panel Adjudications

In festivals not under the auspices of AACT there have never been rules around discussing plays among Adjudicators and often there has been a panel format where all the Adjudicators present their opinions regarding the productions. This allows for more information to be conveyed as there is usually very little repetition and a good idea expressed by one Adjudicator can be elaborated on by the others. Instead of their being three separate timed public presentations of 5 to 7 minutes each there can be 15 to 30 minutes of more detailed discussion about the production.

It is imperative that the Adjudicators understand before they arrive that it will be panel style and who will act as Moderator. If each one is to take on that role then the expectations for the Moderator need to be articulated to everyone in advance. Not everyone will feel comfortable doing this and it is acceptable to have one person among the Adjudicators fulfill the role.

To make these sessions work the Moderator needs to ensure that everyone gets equal time to present thoughts and impressions and that no one goes off on a tangent and monopolizes the time. It works best to have the Moderator rotate the order of presentation because the first person to speak will by definition have the most to talk about and will be providing new information. The Moderator also acts as an informal time keeper being mindful that all subjects are covered and sensing the engagement of the audience.

The Adjudicators should feed off each other and in cases where one may not feel qualified to speak on a certain subject or really does not feel there is anything to say others can take over and fill in. What can happen is that during the discussion the Adjudicator who felt unable to participate fully may pick up on points of the others and elaborate on them. This works well if a production is of poor quality. Sometimes it is hard to know what to say.

In order to moderate well the Adjudicator appointed to that role must listen intently to what the others are saying and be prepared to guide the discussion out of difficult subjects and into a more complete analysis while respecting the views of the other Adjudicators. It is also necessary to deal with conflicting opinions on the same subject which can arise in any adjudication. The difference is, in the panel environment it is immediately apparent and the Moderator has an opportunity to explore it with the others to ensure that the festival participants leave understanding what the reasons for the differing opinions are.

The Moderator can summarize the overall impressions of the team at the end of the allotted time and ensure that the adjudication is positive even if for some reason it has taken on a negative tone.

This kind of dialogue presentation can put the participants more at ease and as well it can foster feedback from them on certain points. It must, of course be well controlled and there is a danger that one Adjudicator will monopolize the proceedings. It is an excellent way to mentor new Adjudicators who can benefit from hearing how a more experienced person approaches the work and what knowledge they bring the festival.

Presentation Summary

Regardless of the format for the adjudication it remains true that the information conveyed needs to be positive, constructive, directed at the performance and not the performer and be educational. It cannot be subjective or negative in tone although it may be critical. For instance, an Adjudicator who tells a performer they are wrong will shut down any discussion or potential for learning by that person and put the rest of the company on alert for potential criticism. Asking a performer or director to consider a different choice gives them the option of considering it but not having to defend what they have done or feeling like they have been attacked. This shows respect for them and the choice made and puts the Adjudicator in the position of appearing to be the one learning rather than it always being the performers who are the students.

It is necessary to remember that Community Theatre is done for love and that all the participants are deeply committed to their work. Being given the opportunity to critique it is a privilege and must be treated with respect. It is possible to make a critical point without condemning the action that led to it or demeaning the performer.

Adjudication is for learning as well as judging and is not a performance opportunity for the Adjudicator. It must always be about the production and the performers and it must leave them encouraged to do more work in the future.

Awards

Award giving is one of the usual requirements of Adjudicators. It can be surrounded by the largest number of pitfalls as emotions run high around winning and even though festivals attempt to stress the educational element over the competitive it is important to people to be recognized among their peers for their work. It is crucial to know what role award giving has in the festival. As an Adjudicator you will be giving awards to suit the requirements of the festival and that may be in conflict with your own attitude about the role of awards in performance. Accepting that the festival organizers have made the decision about what is wanted makes it easier for you to do what is expected.

Early in an Adjudicator's career it is easy to be overwhelmed by the ramifications of choosing one group or individual over another. The potential for criticism on a personal and professional level is high. It is important to remember that the awards given represent the opinion of the Adjudicators and nothing more. All the festival participants will have opinions about who should win what awards and for some half the fun is in second guessing the award giving. How many times do they agree with the Adjudicators' choices? Always remember that awards are a matter of opinion. Hopefully, Adjudicators are giving an educated opinion but it is still only an opinion. It is, however the official one.

There are a number of ways to reduce the potential for problems. The first is to know the festival rules thoroughly and what the criteria are for each award. If it is not necessary to give an award know that in advance. It is not the role of the Adjudicator to comment on the number or kinds of awards to be given or the criteria for winning. Some festivals feel it is necessary for every group to win something. If that is the case it needs to be clear to the participants that this is the decision of the organizers and not the Adjudicators.

Ensure that there is plenty of time for deliberation especially if dialogue around awards will be necessary. The deliberations should remain private. Any person from the festival committee who is present for the deliberation should be used to clarify information like the criteria for the award or performers names etc but not to be an active part of the deliberation. It is critical however, to have someone from the organization present who can vouch for the fairness of the process if indeed there is any question later on. It is not uncommon for this person to need to clarify what exactly an award is for or the history of how it has been given especially if it is an award given in memory or in honor of someone. Ensuring that these special awards are given as they were intended is important.

If it is not required to give all awards then the participants need to know that as well as it sends a message about overall quality if an award is not given. If however, it is an award of a more specific nature like best makeup and there wasn't any makeup used in the productions then it is obvious to everyone that the award does not apply. I once was given the latitude as an Adjudicator to give discretionary awards for "good theatre". There was no requirement to give any such awards and I chose not to. After the festival I was questioned by the organizers as to why I had not give any "good theatre" awards and my response was I did not see any good theatre. The message was very clear.

In order to avoid getting bogged down in the decision making it helps to keep a running tally for yourself of potential winners throughout the festival. The performances are generally broken into segments and after each segment it is important to take the time to note anything in a production that might be worthy of an award. It is easy to forget later if there are a lot of performances and a lot of awards. By noting it during the festival it does not mean it will win just that it will not be overlooked in the consideration and it can always be replaced by something later in the festival that is superior.

A good process to follow while deliberating with other Adjudicators is simply to have one person work as secretary and ask the question "Is there anything in the first production that should be considered for an award based on the awards available?" or to go through the list of awards and ask the question "Is there a person eligible for that award in this production?" Each person can in turn state their opinion without needing to give a reason and it should be noted. If all three have the same idea it is likely to be a winner of something. Two out of three should result in discussion but always allow the majority to rule. It is unusual to have two out of three acknowledge something and the third to have it nowhere for consideration. If that happens then there needs to be a real understanding of why the one Adjudicator found the work was not worthy of an award. If Adjudicators have not been allowed to discuss productions prior to award deliberations they will not have any indication of what the others think unless they have worked together before. It is necessary to take the time to listen to the opinions in order to have each person feel they have had a fair say in the outcome.

Most festivals allow for discretionary awards for the Adjudicators to give out. As a rule it is wise to limit the number of these given otherwise it dilutes the value of them. It starts to look like awards for participation not excellence. These awards should not be used as runner up or consolations for not winning the "big" award.

Discretionary awards should be given to an outstanding element of the production that can not be recognized in any other category. Some examples are original incidental music in a play, a debut performance or a child, exceptional scene painting to name a few. Sometime it is easy to know what to recognize but hard to know what to call it. It is best to avoid calling it best but rather outstanding or excellence in, thus implying its uniqueness and quality.

Often festivals will be very generic in acting awards rather than best actor, best actress etc and give the Adjudicators discretion in giving several acting awards regardless of gender or size of part. That makes it much easier because festivals are not normally balanced in the number of male or female performances and a best of award can eliminate someone from winning who really should be recognized.

If awards are not given by vote or using a point system always keep in mind two criterion. Consider the degree of difficulty of the work and the level of attainment. By keeping these two notions in mind it is possible to differentiate between the quality of performance of very different types of work such as the difference between musicals and comedies.

Often Adjudicators are asked how you can decide between a musical and comedy for instance when selecting a best production award. It always boils down to degree of difficulty and level of attainment. Comedy is not by definition more difficult than musical theatre or drama but if it is a complex comedy requiring a number of different types of comedic skills to be effective and they have all been used on the highest level that needs to be recognized. Equally a sophisticated musical requires a higher level of skill than a simple one piano two singer show with limited musical range. It is not necessary to determine whether comedy is more difficult than musical but it is necessary to fit each of the productions seen into the realm of their genre and judge how successful they are against themselves. Was the comedy fully realized within its genre and was the musical fully realized within its genre?

A fully realized production that works on all levels and meets the playwright's intentions and delivers on all the measurable criteria being used should be awarded the best production over a production of greater complexity and sophistication which does not succeed on all levels. This is where suitability of material comes into play in a large way when assessing the quality of a production. A group can over reach its capability and fail while another group with simpler material can succeed above the merits of the individual piece by doing everything right.

Sometimes it is difficult to give out awards because the overall quality of the festival is poor. In this case always keep in mind that the judgment is relative only to that festival. The "Best of Award" may go to the best of a bad lot but it is still the best. It is not necessary to justify the award choice on any other criteria than what you see.

An Adjudicator should be sure to know how the awards will be presented. Some organizations like the Adjudicators to make the presentations and in others the organizers do it in a way that may have become a tradition for the organization. Regardless, if possible the Adjudicators should be present for the award giving although not front and centre unless involved in the presentation ceremony.

If the Adjudicator is asked to present the awards do not deviate from the presentation process laid out by the organizers. Do no extemporize on the festival quality or the merits of one production over another. Just give out the awards as simply as possible without any editorializing. There can be room for hurt feelings and misunderstanding if something said during the ceremony does not match the outcome. If possible Adjudicators when presenting awards may list the people or productions considered for the award. Just the recognition of having been thought of in the category is uplifting for people. They do not need to know how close they came to winning just that they were considered. It can go a long way especially in a large festival to encouraging people in the future. It is however, the choice of the festival organizers if this will be permitted.

In giving awards rather than announcing the name of the winner first say the name of the show and the character and then the name of the actor because normally there is cheering and applause and it is hard to hear. Not everyone knows everyone at the festival but they will know the production and the character name and can identify the name of the actor later. This also helps if in the worst of all scenarios the wrong person is named. The program could be wrong or a simple mistake is made but the show and character should not be an issue.

Awards are an important responsibility of Adjudicators but they should be a culmination of the process and not the whole exercise. The need to win in competitive festivals is strong. Even if people do not like the Adjudicator they still want the prize. We need to be respectful of that but as an Adjudicator you want to hear from the companies "We did not win but we learned something". That is our measure of success.

Following the awards presentation there are a number of ways to interact with the participants. Some may simply want pictures taken but others may in fact want to engage in conversation with the Adjudicators about the festival and the awards. It is wise to avoid any of this kind of conversation because even though the outcome will not change it is easy to get backed into a corner and say something that can be interpreted differently than it was intended.

Some festivals will have a formal feedback session with the participants after the awards ceremony at which people may ask questions about the adjudications and follow up on points raised during them. This often substitutes for a private adjudication. These sessions can be awkward if the award choices were not popular or obvious. It is possible for the dialogue to become quite subjective while participants attempt to justify what they did. It is not wise to participate in these sessions if all the Adjudicators are not present because the original comments can be taken out of context and one

Adjudicator should not comment on the opinions of another especially if they have not heard the original adjudication.

Above all when giving awards do not feel guilty about the choices made. It is all a matter of opinion and no two people at the festival will agree on the award choices. Adjudicators are asked to give awards in what may be unusual categories or which may not in fact represent what happened at the festival. That is the decision of the festival committee and the Adjudicator is charged with following the guidelines. As long as the Awards are treated with respect and to the best of everyone's ability reflect the level of excellence at the festival that is all that is required.

Issues that may Arise

Besides the obvious challenges of maintaining objectivity during a festival when faced with differing quality in productions and scripts being presented, there are other issues which may creep into the mix.

Many times Adjudicators inadvertently become involved in the politics of the organizations. This can happen in a number of ways. Giving an unbiased critical adjudication of a performance to a company known for producing high quality plays and traditionally winning is one. The festival will be instantly abuzz.

Prior association or knowledge of a group or individuals can be perceived as favoritism especially when awards are to be given. I remember adjudicating a festival at which my home theatre company was performing and although I had been assured by the festival committee that it would not be a problem after the company had performed the gossip started that they would win because I was a member of the company. The director of the play upon hearing it is reported to have said "I guess you were not listening to the adjudication. She hated it" and I had.

Adjudicators are sometimes asked to comment on the festival organization and the rules being followed. It is the best policy to avoid this and if pressed to do so refuse to comment until the festival is over and then only to those officially in charge and only if asked. Sometimes an Adjudicator who has attended the same festival a number of times may be asked if they see any change in the quality of the work. Hopefully the answer is that it is improving but if it is not then when asked it is appropriate to say so in order for the festival committee to understand where they stand. Do not compare one festival to another unless making a procedural suggestion. Sometimes an Adjudicator can offer insight into how to solve a logistical problem because it has been overcome at another festival.

Don't complain, but if there are things that happened that made it difficult to adjudicate properly like lack of breaks between shows, poor scheduling, lack of clear instructions etc it is appropriate to say so in order to improve things the next time. Do not comment on the skills of your fellow Adjudicators. It is not fair and is gossipy and hurtful. You do not want them talking about you so refrain from doing it about them.

Issues can arise around censorship and copyright. The rules of copyright and the handling of violations are the responsibility of the festival. Normally rules are published which require that copyright be adhered to and proof of royalties having been paid in advance of the performance. Any issues around this do not affect the adjudication but an Adjudicator may question if approval has been obtained for changes made to a script. Sometimes plays that are in the public domain, meaning royalties no longer apply and copyright no longer exists can be changed significantly. An Adjudicator needs to know if permission was required and obtained before commenting on alterations. It is still valid to comment on the quality of the changes even if permission has been given by the playwright or in some cases the playwright has provided the new version.

Censorship is a more sensitive issue which can result in touchy situations. Groups may choose to alter a script due to content but it often leads to questionable productions because so much of the essence of the script has been removed. That is something for the Adjudicator to comment upon as it affects the ability of the company to produce a fully realized production but they should not express a point of view about censorship as a practice. Remember you do not have to live there when the festival is over. In some places censorship is practiced openly and unapologetically as being the right of the performers or company. These kinds of value judgments are entirely subjective and therefore unassailable. It is best to address only the choices made with respect to how they alter the playwright's intention from a purely dramaturgical point of view. To discuss it on any other level is poison.

Personalities of committee members or participating groups are also areas that can cause problems. Some people may have a long history of animosity with others and it should never be discussed in your presence. If it is then by all means do not participate in the discussion even if you have an opinion. An Adjudicator must never give the appearance of taking sides in a political issue.

Sometimes the behavior of a fellow Adjudicator is less than professional. Once again this should never be a discussion point with anyone. The organizers must handle the problem. On one occasion a fellow Adjudicator took offense at something said during the award deliberations. He chose to make his displeasure public. Although I agreed with his position I did not agree with his action regarding it. The organizers asked me to confirm what had happened which I did but I did not comment on his response. Providing facts is one thing but providing opinion is quite another. Stay out of any discussions that do not pertain directly to the adjudications whenever possible. Remember you are a guest of the festival and you should always act like one.

Other Types of Festivals

The forgoing pages have described in detail the role of an Adjudicator in the most common kind of festivals in North America, competitive single language festivals. There are other kinds of festivals where an Adjudicator will have a role. Two that come to mind are multi language festivals and new play festivals. In both cases the basic principles remain the same but there are other issues which come into play.

International Festivals

In multi language festivals the most obvious difference is that the Adjudicators are not able to understand the language of every play. The productions are being presented in the language chosen by the performing company and are playing before a multilingual audience most of whom will not understand the text. In order to be successful in these environments an Adjudicator needs to focus on understanding the production on a broader level and allow the entire theatrical experience to happen. This means that the language becomes secondary to the acting, directing and visual elements etc. Each of these components becomes even more critical to the audience's ability to understand what the playwright wants us to know.

A good synopsis of the plot is necessary if a copy of the play is not available in the language of the Adjudicator. This will allow the Adjudicator to have a reference point for what is happening on the stage. If what has been described as the action does not appear to be happening on the stage and is not easily identifiable, then the theatrical elements are not supporting the production.

If the actors are not creating the natural progression of the characters and the situation, then again they are not supporting the play. If they are not able to maintain the audience's interest even without the language then the acting is not of high quality.

These two components are equally important when adjudicating productions in your own language but it is easy to allow the words to do the work that the theatrics should be doing. It is a good lesson for adjudicating any theatre to watch as if you do not understand the words.

Communication is 80% non verbal. Language can be allowed to take its place in theatre but it does not have to be the main focus. It is amazing how much more we can see and understand if the language is eliminated. Theatre is theatre no matter where you are and that is never clearer than when adjudicating an International festival.

An Adjudicator must simply forget about trying to understand the words and rather concentrate on the action on the stage. It is not dissimilar to watching the opera minus the Surtitles. If you allow it to happen as a total experience it will. It takes practice and enormous concentration to work this way but it is highly rewarding.

Production values become very important when watching theatre in a language you do not understand. If props, costumes, setting etc do not tell you something specific then your confusion will be compounded. Each element of the theatre needs to be highly developed.

There is so much to be learned from watching the theatrical experience and traditions of other countries. The Japanese, for instance produce highly visual productions which often rely on precise movement and strong stage pictures to convey the story. South American countries tend to produce theatre that is highly dramatic and focused on political tension and often use strong metaphors to convey their feelings about life. The plays tend to be tense and emotional and deeply moving. Understanding the theatrical traditions of a country can be helpful. Having adjudicated two productions of Chinese opera I know I only have 498 more types to learn about. What I do know, and is common in all forms of their opera is the Chinese love of spectacle and the use of myth, legend and fairy tales to tell their stories.

Whenever possible an Adjudicator going to an International festival should find out as much as possible about the traditions of the countries performing before going as it will help to create a context for evaluation. Do not be intimidated by the traditions of other countries. Remember this is all Community Theatre and just because it came to a festival does not mean it is good.

When presenting the adjudication at an International festival there are some considerations that must be kept in mind. Just like the audience not being able to understand the language of the play many will not be able to understand the Adjudicator without translation and to be successful you must change the nature of your presentation. The basic principles still apply as to clarity of ideas, simplicity and positive communication however beyond this it is necessary to ensure that the ideas being expressed can be clearly understood in translation. In order to facilitate translation either by official translators or audience members translating for each other ensure your language is simple and speak slowly. Use less complicated metaphors or analogies and speak as directly to your point as possible. Do not tell convoluted stories as illustrations of your point or rely on sophisticated language. Humor is difficult to translate and frustrating for the audience who will not get the joke until after the laughter of those who understood you.

When speaking about the production remember the cultural differences of the performing country and particularly those of the host country. Most of your audience will have a particular experience and you should try to explain your point of view relative to their understanding. Give them examples of how something works theatrically and why it heightens understanding of the play. Particularly speak to visual elements of the production as well as emotions and actions of the characters and how they conveyed the playwright's intent to you.

There is a balance in the International festival environment between critiquing "theatrically" and helping the audience to access the production based on what you saw and can explain to them. You are teaching on a different level. It must be meaningful to the participants but also to the audience who may need to learn how to watch theatre from other cultures and in other languages and can feel intimidated by the experience. A good Adjudicator can make the festival more enjoyable for everyone.

Many International festivals are not competitive but the Adjudicator can still be a valuable part of the experience by making audience education even more the focus.

New Play Festivals

Festivals are starting to emerge that are focused on new plays. One of the reasons for this is the ability of Community Theatres to produce unproven plays when Professional companies may not be willing to take the financial risk. The new play festivals are not only focused on adjudication of the production but often allow for discussion about the play itself.

In this environment Adjudicators are encouraged to comment on how the script has worked. Sometimes new scripts have incomplete character development and that makes it hard for actors to really establish anything more then the basic narrative line of the story. This is often true because an inexperienced playwright will focus first on telling the story and then on developing character. Because it is not a novel the character development cannot be conveyed by description but must be written as dialogue. Playwrights will sometimes resort to a lot of narration to tell the audience what it is going to see rather than showing us through character interaction what it happening. This may be because it is cheaper to produce plays with fewer characters so the playwright is writing to suit that or because creating more characters is more complicated and writing realistic dialogue is difficult. Plays at new play festivals are often works in progress and feedback about the shortcomings is usually part of the adjudication process.

An informal adjudication works well for these kinds of festivals as it allows for feedback from the actors and playwrights with the Adjudicator acting as moderator to guide the discussion. The discussion is meant to encourage dialogue that will help the playwright to see ways the script needs to be changed in order to be a successful play. It is necessary to distinguish between problems within the play and problems with the production and to offer solutions for the issues raised. Once again it is not advisable to show prejudice to a script or to reveal likes and dislikes, rather the Adjudicator needs to encourage development of the material.

Often new play festivals allow productions that are not complete such as book in hand, staged readings or minimal production values added to the presentation. The purpose is to focus on the play rather than the performance but the Adjudicator needs to be able to differentiate between performance and script shortcomings even if all production values are not completely developed. It is still possible to distinguish the difference between problems in the writing and potential performance problems.

It can be a challenge when a festival is a combination of new and proven works. The new plays may in fact not be of the quality of the published plays and suffer by comparison because of that. Adjudicators need to be clear on what the festival mandate is. If a company chooses to present a new play in a more established festival environment that is their choice and they need to be held to the same production standards as any other presentation.

Conclusion

Adjudication can offer a tremendous learning experience for audiences and performers. It can help to enlighten everyone about different types of theatre and it should challenge everyone to improve. At its best it can raise the level of the work being presented and stimulate people to do better with future productions.

Adjudication requires knowledge about the theatre, good presentation skills and most importantly a passion for teaching and critiquing work in an environment of respect and growth for all involved. It is important too that people wanting to be Adjudicators understand that it is a separate skill from their already acquired skills as directors, actors and teachers and that it will take time and practice as well as study to learn to do it well.

It can be rewarding and fun combined with hard work but it will ultimately make anyone who chooses to become an Adjudicator better at their own theatrical work as well. It will provide a lifetime of learning and an opportunity to be exposed to plays and productions that you might not otherwise ever see and to learn from them how to create better productions.

In writing this book I have learned that there is much about adjudication that is subjective and always open to interpretation, but there are some basic principles that if adhered to will make for a good experience for both the participants and the Adjudicators. After more than 25 years adjudicating festivals, I can say I continue to look forward to the next one with as much pleasure and wonder as I have every other one I have adjudicated in the past.

See you at the Theatre.

Annette G. Procunier has been active in theatre for 40 years starting, as so many do with her high school play. She is a graduate of the University of Toronto.

As well as being an acclaimed director she is in great demand as a teacher of adjudication and directing in addition to her role as an Adjudicator. Annette is admired for her clarity, sense of humour and passion for the theatre as well as her ability to engage festival participants in exploring all elements of production. She has adjudicated more than 100 festivals in North America, Europe and Asia during the past 26 years.

She is a member of the Theatre Ontario Talent Bank and the American Association of Community Theatres. In 2009 Annette was made a fellow of AACT for "single handedly raising the level of Community Theatre in America". She is the only non American to ever receive this lifetime award.

CPSIA information can be obtained at www.ICGtesting.com
Printed in the USA
LVOW13s2236260214

375281LV00002B/462/P